The
Big Book of
John Deere
Tractors

The Complete Model-by-Model
Encyclopedia, Plus Classic Toys,
Brochures, and Collectibles

By Don Macmillan

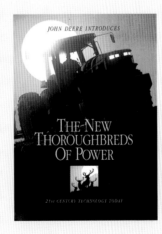

Foreword by
Harold L. Brock,
John Deere Tractor
Designer 1959–1985

Photographs by
Andrew Morland
and
Randy Leffingwell

Voyageur Press

First published in 2010 by Voyageur Press, an imprint of MBI Publishing Company,
400 First Avenue North, Suite 300, Minneapolis, MN 55401 USA

To find out more about our books, visit us online at www.voyageurpress.com.

ISBN-13: 978-0-7603-3653-3

Editor: Michael Dregni
First edition designer: Andrea Rud
Cover designed by: Rob Johnson

Printed in China

On the front cover: *A classic Styled John Deere Model A in front of a late-model Deere.* Lee Klancher
On the endpapers: *A 1937 Model A.*
On the frontispiece, top: *A pre-production 9300T with 1810 chisel plow.*
Right bottom: *A Waterloo Boy advertisement.*
Left bottom: *A farmer resting on the hood of his trusty Deere. (Library of Congress)*
On the title page, main: *While Dad eats his lunch, Junior and Spot pretend they are piloting the family's "Poppin' Johnny" in this painting by artist Walter Haskell Hinton.*
Inset: *"The New Thoroughbreds of Power" brochure announced the 8000 Series in 1994.*
On the contents page: *A 1920s Deere Model GP advertisement.*

Contents

Foreword

By Harold L. Brock
Ford N Series tractor design engineer 1939–1958
Deere & Company New Generation tractor engineering executive 1959–1985
Society of Automotive Engineers president 1971

I was privileged to have been asked in 1959 by Mr. William Hewitt, then the rather new chairman of Deere & Company, to join his organization to help develop a new line of tractors. Mr. Hewitt's earlier experiences as a territory manager of Ford tractor marketing had made him acquainted with the 9N, 2N, and 8N tractor projects under my control at Ford. My admiration of Deere's management style and engineering experience convinced me to join ranks to help Deere accomplish its position of leadership.

This book delineates the typical search of most full-line farm equipment companies to serve the needs of their farm customers. John Deere built its business by acquiring various equipment manufacturers. In doing so, much nonuniformity existed and many of these products carried their previous identities. Deere's dedicated effort, to work with their farm customers to better serve their needs resulted in great strides in reducing the labor and drudgery of producing farm commodities. More importantly, this built a strong dealer organization and farm customer relationship of lasting value.

Above: *A 1935 Deere Model B tractor pulls a No. 10 Deere corn picker near Dell Rapids, South Dakota. (Deere & Company archives)*

Facing page: *Like father, like son: Love for farm tractors can begin at a dangerously young age, as this painting by artist Walter Haskell Hinton suggests. Dad takes time out from spring plowing with his Model D to oil the axle bearings on junior's own homemade Deere tractor.*

Deere & Company management under Mr. Hewitt's leadership had determined in the mid-1950s that a more aggressive approach was needed to update its line of tractors if the firm was to be a leader in the industry. At the time, the company had several styles of tractors produced by different factories, and components and features of the products differed. Proliferation of unique parts existed in the line of tractors, and customer acceptance of differing features between products created confusion. To overcome these problems, management established a new product engineering center at Waterloo, Iowa, and assigned key engineers to create a completely new line of product.

Henry Dreyfuss Associates of New York City had worked with Deere factories to create a family of products easily identified by their excellence of detail. The attention to ergonomics and human factors helped create greater operator comfort, and these products incorporated many new firsts in the industry for customer comfort and ease of operation. Farm customers recognized the radical change from the older line of product and gradually accepted the new concepts. With the acceptance of the new concepts, the rest of the line of tractors was brought into a family of products. By doing so, proliferation of designs and unique parts were reduced. Family features and functional components between products complemented each other instead of competing. By the mid-1960s, Deere had become a leader of the industry.

With the introduction of new products, Deere became a leader in developing worldwide designs and drawings that could be used in both metric and English units of measurement, which permitted Deere to produce worldwide without conversion of drawings. Most major industries have now adopted this concept. Continual updating of product features such as Roll-Gard, quiet safety cabs, enhanced operator comfort, and new standards of highway lighting, has kept Deere in a leadership role.

Deere's global marketing was extended under Mr. Hewitt's leadership. In addition, greater efforts were made to enhance Deere's corporate identity. A glorious corporate headquarters building was built in Moline, Illinois, and all marketing functions and facilities were updated to reflect a greater quality image.

Don Macmillan has very ably organized a historical record of the many product attempts of Deere & Company to become the farm equipment industry leader. As you progress through the book, you will observe how the tractor industry has evolved into a more standardized family of products. Major milestones such as the use of herbicides that reduced the need for front cultivators, the adoption of standardized three-point hitches for implement attachment, and more have resulted in more uniformity of chassis configuration. As the ever-increasing

application of new science and technology is applied to design concepts, more standardization can be expected. This should benefit the farm customer just as the adoption of the three-point hitch for implements eliminated the need for purchasing new equipment when changing product lines.

The sun sets on a 1935 Model BN. Owner: Frank Bettencourt, Vernalis, California, USA. (Photograph © Randy Leffingwell)

In the Beginning

The story of the gasoline-powered farm tractor stretches back more than a century to the machine that pioneering engineer John Froelich built in 1892. The visionary foresight of Froelich was inherited by Deere & Company. Over the past one hundred years, Deere has developed a long lineage of farm tractors, beginning with Froelich's early creation and continuing on to the current Thousand Series tractors in the famous green-and-yellow garb. Today, Deere is the largest manufacturer of farm machinery in the world.

My story with John Deere began in March 1940. I worked on a British farm of 640 acres (256 hectares), or 1 square mile (2.6 sq km), and our only tractor when World War II started was a 15-hp Allis-Chalmers Model B. The rest of the work on this farm, made up of arable land and two dairy operations, was done with horses and the annual visit of a custom steam threshing outfit. We needed to plow more land, so a new Allis WF was ordered. The delivery was delayed, however, and a new John Deere AR was offered instead. We accepted the Deere subject to a successful demonstration on a steep field we were about to reclaim. As one of the farm's tractor drivers—three of us kept the Allis B working twenty-four hours a day to cope with the wartime demands—I was the driver chosen for the demonstration. The tractor passed its test with flying colors, and I was thus instantly converted from an "orange" enthusiast to one of "green and yellow."

Above: *Don Macmillan pilots Wayne Aigner's three-speed Model D at the 1991 Rollag, Minnesota, show.*

Facing page: *Model AW wide-front. Owner: Don Wolf of Indiana, USA. (Photograph © Andrew Morland)*

On the gas tank of the new tractor was a decal that read, "John Deere, Moline, Ill.," so I wrote a letter to that address extolling the virtues of the AR. In a short time, I received a reply with an invitation to visit Moline "after the war is over."

On August 1, 1942, I started custom plowing and other work for farmers. No new or used Deere tractors were available to purchase in England, so I had to make do with an Oliver 90 and a Ransomes four-bottom Multitrac plow. With a rapidly growing market for my custom work during World War II, I applied to the local War Agricultural Committee for a new Deere Model D and was allocated one. February 8, 1943, marked the arrival of the new D, serial number 154757. It was the first of many Johnny Poppers that I owned and used over the next few years.

The resulting association between myself and Deere was cemented when I first visited the United States in September 1947. I toured Deere's headquarters in Moline, which were downtown at that time; the East Moline Harvester works; and the Waterloo, Iowa, and newly opened Dubuque, Iowa, tractor factories. Even here fate decreed that, as the only plowman in the party of overseas visitors, I would have to demonstrate the new Model M and its two-bottom integral plow.

While visiting Moline, I wanted to spend a day on one of the first Model 55 combines and traveled to Champaign, Illinois, where the closest 55 was working in soybeans. The event foreshadowed my ownership of the only two 55 combines imported to England the following year.

In 1958, I was appointed the first Deere dealer in the United Kingdom and, in 1959, made a second visit to the United States.

The other abiding memory of that trip was a visit, again with Bob Lovett, to Marshalltown, Iowa, for the largest—and last—display of two-cylinder 30 Series tractors. This show also marked the announcement of the giant 8010 tractor with its integral eight-bottom plow, a portent of the future.

It was through a fortunate series of coincidences that I was present at these auspicious moments: the first year of Deere's self-propelled combine era, 1947; the 1947 opening of the Dubuque factory; the end of the John Deere two-cylinder line in 1959; and the beginning, as then yet unsuspected, of Deere's multi-cylinder tractor era. These events were all building blocks in the formation of the world's Number One farm machinery company.

A young Deere convert gets the hang of his new 3140 pedal tractor.

CHAPTER 1

JOHN FROELICH.

The Pioneering Years, 1892–1924

Above: *Pioneering Iowa engineer John Froelich designed the world's first tractor capable of propelling itself forward and backward.*

Left: *John Deere looks on with pride as a farmer uses the Deere & Company Gilpin Sulky Plow in this painting. The Deere works at Moline, Illinois, are in the background.*

Froelich Tractor and Waterloo Boy
Models TP and P, 1892–1913

Deere & Company's farm tractor history began indirectly in Waterloo, Iowa, in 1892, when pioneering engineer John Froelich built his first "tractor," a term not then in use. Froelich's creation was powered by a crude gasoline-fueled, internal-combustion engine and successfully propelled itself both forwards and backwards. From this early—and not entirely auspicious—beginning, the Waterloo Gasoline Engine Company was founded.

Froelich was inspired to create his tractor as an alternative to the steam traction engines of the late nineteenth century. Farmers in the Dakotas were stymied in their use of steamers as wood or coal was not easily available there. Froelich purchased a gas-fueled, 20-hp stationary engine from the Van Duzen firm of Cincinnati, Ohio. With the help of William Mann, a blacksmith in his home town, they mounted the engine on a wood frame. Using components obtained from the steam-engine builder, Robinson and Company, Froelich and Mann built the first gas-engined traction capable of powering itself forwards and backwards.

As with so many inventions, Froelich's first tractor proved to be ahead of its time. He built four more trac-

tors but was not satisfied with them. Although he continued to experiment, the Waterloo Gasoline Engine Company only survived for its first eighteen years by building its Waterloo Boy stationary engine line.

In 1911, the firm returned to the tractor business and, after years of development, produced a reliable tractor, the Model R, that was both inexpensive and simple to operate and maintain, making it ideal for the farmers of the day, who were inexperienced with operating the new-fangled machinery. This first tractor was advertised as the Waterloo Boy One Man Tractor with the Practical Plow Hitch; this Model TP Four-Cylinder Standard Wheel model was introduced for larger farms. It was powered by a cross-mounted, L-head, four-cycle, water-cooled engine with a bore and stroke of 5.50x6.00 inches (137.5x150 mm). The Model TP featured two forward and one reverse speeds, automotive-style steering, and a mounted plow with four 14-inch (35-cm) bottoms and power lift.

A version of the Model TP was introduced in 1913 with Caterpillar-style tracks and called variously the Sure Grip, Never Slip, and Model P. As an advertisement of the day noted, it was sold "at a price that is within the reach of every farmer who owns 160 acres of good land."

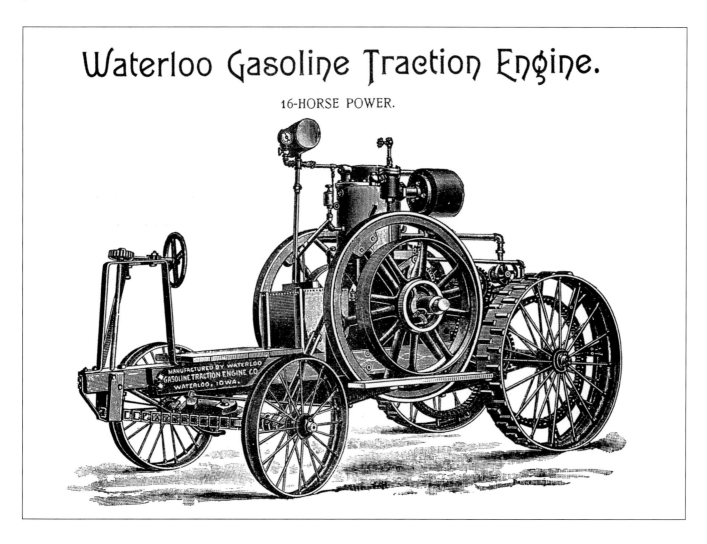

Above: *A 1/16-scale model of the Froelich tractor made by Scale Models of Dyersville, Iowa, USA. Scale Models was started in 1978 by Joe Ertl, son of Ertl Company founder Fred Ertl.*

The Only Gasoline Traction Engine
···ON EARTH.···

The **Waterloo**
+ Gasoline +
+ Traction +
+ Engine. +

···· MANUFACTURED BY ····

The Waterloo Gasoline Traction Engine Co.,
WATERLOO, IOWA, U. S. A.

The cover of the original Froelich brochure.

Above: *A replica of the Froelich tractor built by workers at the Waterloo, Iowa, tractor works in 1937. The Froelich replica was on display at Deere's Moline administration center.*

Facing page: *A drawing of the Froelich tractor from the original brochure.*

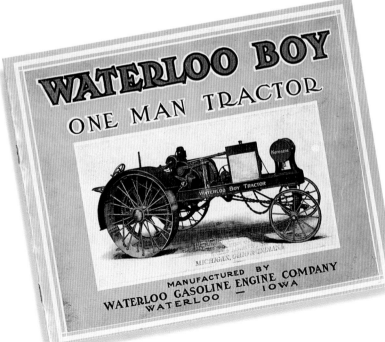

Above: *This Model R Style G, number 1568, is the oldest known Waterloo Boy. It has the L-head motor and the small-diameter dual kerosene gas tank. The radiator was positioned on the right side; it was soon moved to the left to improve driver vision. Owner: Travis Jorde.*

Left: *The 1914 Waterloo Boy brochure with the tractor illustrated on the cover.*

Waterloo Boy Models L, LA, C, H, R, and N, 1913–1924

Later in 1913, the Model L, or Light Tractor, was added to the Waterloo Boy line. The L featured a mounted two-bottom plow and was powered by a horizontally opposed, two-cylinder engine of 6.00x6.00 inches (150x150 mm) that produced 15 hp at 500 rpm. Records show that twenty-nine Model L and LA tractors were delivered during 1914.

Advertisements of the day indicate that two other models were also offered. The Model C tractor used the same engine as the L but featured all-wheel drive. The larger, 25-hp Model H featured a 7.00x7.00-inch (175x175-mm) two-cylinder opposed engine running at 450 rpm. The H weighed 6,500 pounds (2,925 kg) compared with the 3,000 pounds (1,350 kg) of the L, and both models had automobile-type steering and forward speeds of 2–2¼ mph (3.2–3.6 kph) for plowing and 3 mph (4.8 kph).

During 1914, a new model was developed with a twin-cylinder, side-by-side engine that was to become the standard engine style of Waterloo Boy and Deere tractors for the next forty-six years. The predecessor of the lineage was the Waterloo Boy Model R.

From 1914 to 1917, the Model R appeared in twelve different styles: The first four, styles A through D, had 5.50x7.00-inch (137.5x175-mm) L-head motors; the next seven styles, E through L, had an increased bore of 6.00 inches (150 mm); the final style, M, had a 6.50x7.00-inch (162.5x175-mm) engine. Strangely, the Model R was fitted with a single forward speed and chain steering, which was seemingly a step backwards in progress.

The two-speed Model N was introduced in 1917, and finally acquired automotive-style steering in 1920 together with other modifications, including a higher fuel tank position and a riveted frame. In 1924, concurrent with production of the Deere Model D tractor, ninety-three Model N tractors were built to use up existing parts, and numbered from 31320 to 31412.

Below, top: *Waterloo Boy Model R Style H, number 2512. Note the left-hand radiator, larger-diameter kerosene-only tank, and red engine color.*

Below, bottom: *Waterloo Boy Model N, number 28629, with riveted frame and auto steering, found by the author in Canada in August 1978, and purchased in January 1980. Present owner Brian Davey restored the tractor.*

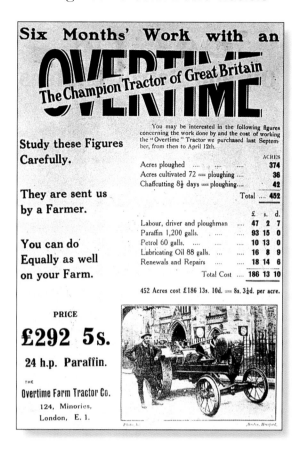

Above: *A World War I–era advertisement for "The Champion Tractor of Great Britain," the Overtime R, showing its cost of operation for plowing, cultivating, and on belt work.*

Overtime Models R and N, 1916–1919

Due to the German submarine threat to the food supply of Great Britain during World War I, the Waterloo works sold some 4,000 Model R and chain-steer N tractors to L. J. Martin's Overtime Farm Tractor Company of London. These machines were shipped in crates, assembled in the British company's London works, and painted in the firm's own color scheme of orange wheels, dark green frame and fenders, and gunmetal-gray fuel tank, engine, and radiator.

Advertisements in *Implement and Tractor*, the British farm machinery trade journal, dated from September 1, 1915, to the end of 1918, show the tractor in its various styles from the early right-hand-radiator model to the vertical-fuel-tank Model R versions through to the 1919 Model N two-speed tractor still fitted with chain steering.

In 1919, Martin changed the name of his company to Associated Manufacturers' Company but retained the same Minories address in London and the Overtime Tractor Department. This firm later became importers of J. I. Case farm machinery.

The earliest known surviving Overtime Model R—and the only one shown in the work's records with two serial numbers, 1728 and 1747. In the records, under "1728" it says "see 1747," which was shipped to L. J. Martin of London. Owner: the Lackham Museum, part of the Wiltshire Agricultural College, Lacock, Wiltshire, England.

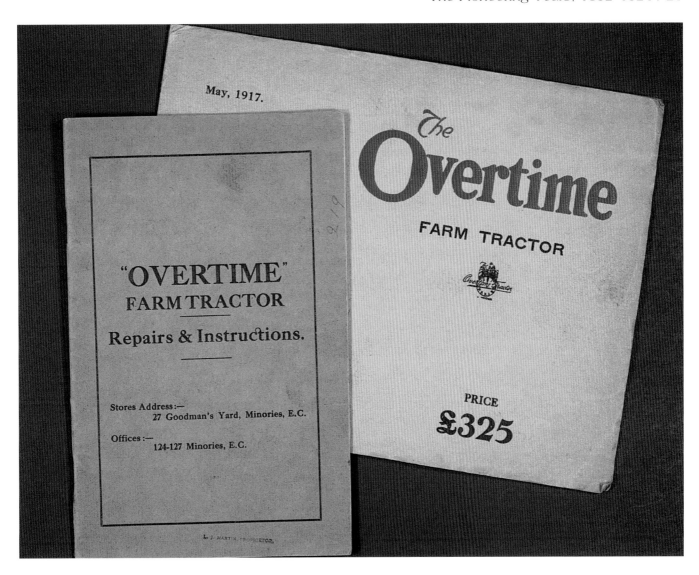

Above: *May 1917 sales brochure and parts book for the Overtime R stamped with the address of dealer Messrs. Edward W. Maundrell of Calne, Wiltshire, England.*

Left: *A replica of the Waterloo Boy Model R by the Ertl Company of Dyersville, Iowa, USA, follows the Style H form.*

Above: *A 1916 Overtime. Owners: Walter and Bruce Keller of Kaukauna, Wisconsin, USA. (Photograph © Randy Leffingwell)*

Right: *The Ertl replica of the Overtime R.*

Above, top: *An Overtime supplied by Maundrell of Calne, England, at work plowing on Charles Vines's farm near Calne during World War I. Vines is on the tractor, his wife on the plow.*

Above, bottom: *A World War I–era photo of an Overtime pulling two binders in East Anglia, England.*

Right: *The 1919 Overtime N brochure, while appearing to make optimistic claims for its horsepower, was proud to proclaim it "The Champion Tractor of England and Wales."*

THE NEW 30-H.P.
Overtime

NATIONAL
FOOD PRODUCTION
CAMPAIGN

CHAMPION TRACTOR
OF
ENGLAND
AND
WALES

WON BY THE OVERTIME TRACTOR

TWO-SPEED
FARM TRACTOR
1919 MODEL. "N."

Deere Tractor Prototypes and All-Wheel-Drive Tractor, 1910–1918

With the rising popularity of the gas-powered tractor, Deere came under increasing pressure from some of its branch houses to get into the tractor business. After a prolonged boardroom battle, Deere management began the search for a tractor to complete its line of farm machinery.

As early as 1910, some Deere branch houses sold the massive Big Four Model 30 tractor from the Gas Traction Company of Minneapolis, Minnesota. The Big Four 30 won a gold medal at the 1910 Winnipeg, Canada, trials pulling a seven-bottom 14-inch (35-cm) Deere gang plow. At the same time, Deere's export department listed the Minneapolis Steel & Machinery Company's Twin City Model 40 tractor in Argentina and Uruguay for use with its gang plows.

The board of directors therefore resolved on March 5, 1912, to "produce a tractor plow," and Deere staff engineer C. H. Melvin was instructed to build an experimental model. Melvin's prototype tractor bore a resemblance to the Hackney Auto-Plow of St. Paul, Minnesota, but never entered production.

By May 1914, Joseph Dain, Sr., who joined the board when Deere purchased his hay machinery company in 1910, was put in charge of producing a tractor that could be sold for $700. The culmination of Dain's experiments was a decision in 1917 to build one hundred of his final design, and these were the first tractors to carry the Deere company name. To date, two of these All-Wheel-Drive models have survived along with parts of a third.

In the end, however, the Dain tractors had to be priced at more than twice the original $700 estimate, and thus never sold as well as hoped. Their specifications did include drive to all the wheels and an automatic gearbox, options that would not be commonly available on other tractors for nearly fifty years.

In March 1918, four months after the decision to build the Dain AWD, Deere purchased the Waterloo Gasoline Tractor Company. Deere thus acquired an accepted tractor model, which was selling at half the proposed cost of the new deluxe Dain machine.

The performance of the AWD tractors appears to have been all that the designers had hoped for. The Dain's demise in preference for the simple Waterloo Boy two-cylinder models was based on cost and the capacity of farmers of the day to appreciate the added sophistication of the AWD. In hindsight, the decision to change course and continue to produce the Waterloo design seemed inevitable.

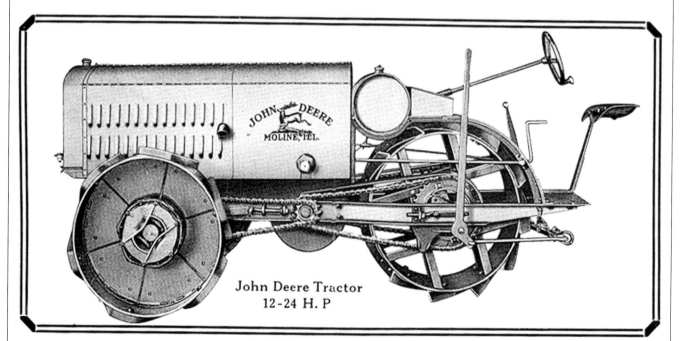

JOHN DEERE TRACTOR

John Deere Tractor
12-24 H. P

The All-Wheel-Drive Tractor

Above: *An original All-Wheel-Drive tractor brochure.*

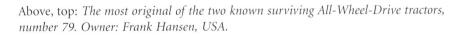

Above, top: *The most original of the two known surviving All-Wheel-Drive tractors, number 79. Owner: Frank Hansen, USA.*

Above, bottom: *Big 4 Model 30 tractor as built by the Gas Traction Company of Minneapolis, Minnesota, and sold by certain Deere branch houses from 1910 on.*

Facing page: *An outline drawing of the All-Wheel-Drive tractor from the original brochure.*

The second known surviving All-Wheel-Drive tractor, number 34. Originally owned by Len Williams, who left it to the Northern Illinois Steam Power Club, DeKalb, Illinois, USA.

One of the numbered, 1/16-scale models of the All-Wheel-Drive tractor; 1,000 of these were commissioned by Frank Hansen.

The All-Wheel-Drive tractor Instruction Book and Repair List.

Lanz Landbaumotor LB, LC, LCM, and LD; Bulldog HL, HP, and Felddank, 1911–1926

Tractor development was also taking place at the same time on the other side of the Atlantic. The evolution of one particular tractor builder—Heinrich Lanz of Mannheim, Germany—would come to play an essential role in Deere & Company.

Born in 1838, just a year after John Deere crafted his first steel plow, Heinrich Lanz started his business by importing steam engines and threshing machines from England. He soon began to build both engines and threshers in Germany, and his works in Mannheim were established in 1859; by the time Deere purchased Lanz in 1956, the works covered 118 acres (47.2 hectares). Threshers, mills, presses, and chaff cutters were all in production when steam engines were added in 1879.

Lanz visited the United States in 1902, where he met Charles Deere, the son of John Deere. The meeting inspired Lanz's enthusiasm for further mechanization, but it was left to his son, Karl Lanz, to see these dreams to fruition.

In 1911, Lanz acquired the license to build the Koszegi motor-drawn rotovator, which had been designed in 1907. Also in 1911, Lanz built its first-style Landbaumotor LB, or "field-working machine." The Landbaumotor and the firm's steam engines were widely exported, with up to 40 percent of production going to Russia; when World War I started, all exports ceased, never to return. Updated models of the Landbaumotor were added, including the LC of 1914–1917, the LCM of 1917–1918, and the LD of 1919–1926.

Lanz wartime production included twenty-two airships built in Leipzig and five hundred airplanes from Mannheim. When Karl Lanz returned from the war, he focused on developing a new agricultural tractor, resulting in 1921 in the legendary Bulldog. Designed by Dr. Fritz Huber, the Bulldog was the world's first hot-bulb-fired, crude-oil-burning tractor, and would inspire a long line and numerous models of famous machines.

In 1923, several new models were introduced. An articulated, four-wheel-drive version of the original Bulldog Model HL, known as the Acker-Bauern HP Bulldog, was launched. The Felddank 38-hp model also made its debut in 1923 with a vertical two-cylinder benzine-fueled motor, three forward speeds, and automobile-type steering. The Felddank was capable of pulling a three- or four-bottom plow. Both of these models were built until 1926, when the new HR2 Gross Bulldog replaced the early crude-oil models.

Top left: *Works illustration of a 1915 Landbaumotor LC. The first Landbaumotor, the LB, debuted in 1911; the last, the LD, was launched in 1926.*

Top right: *Heinrich and Karl Lanz.*

Above: *Lanz 12-hp HL Bulldog tractor, number 2003. Previous owner: Sir Neville Bowman-Shaw, Toddington Manor Museum, Bedfordshire, England.*

Right: *An original HL Bulldog brochure.*

BULLDOG

Heavy oil engine.

WATERLOO BOY T

BURNS KEROSENE COMPL

Points of Merit

1. **Simple Design**—easy to understand—you can expert it yourself.
2. **Burns Kerosene.** Patented manifold gasifies the kerosene and saves many dollars in fuel cost every year. No kerosene to work past piston rings into crank case to destroy quality of lubricating oil and result in burning out bearings.
3. **Powerful Two-Cylinder Engine** delivers its full rated 25 horse-power on belt and 12 horse-power on draw-bar.
4. **Heavy Two-Throw Balanced Crank Shaft**—long-lived motor and increased power due to lack of vibration.
5. **Simple and Positive Oiling System**—automatic—extremely low oil consumption.
6. **Water Cooled** by large core radiator. Capacity of cooling system, 13 gallons. Water circulated by reliable centrifugal pump.
7. **Reliable Ignition**—simple high tension magneto with impulse starter.
8. **Extra Strong Gears,** case-hardened, heat-treated, dust-proof, run in oil.
9. **Roller Bearings** at all important points reduce friction and conserve power.
10. **Right-Hand Drive Wheel in Furrow**—a big advantage in plowing—prevents side draft on plow and tractor. Self-steering.
11. **Pulley Driven Direct** from engine crank shaft—a big advantage in belt work—no gears in mesh—every ounce of power utilized.
12. **Low Repair Cost** and John Deere repair service.

Pulling a John Deere 3-bottom plow. Drive wheel in furrow—no plow or tractor side draft.

Pulling John Deere Heavy Tractor Disc Harrow and Brillion Pulverizer—good seed beds rapidly.

Pulling two John Deere 8-foot b harvesting done at the ri

WATERLOO BOY

JOHN DEERE
MOLINE·ILL.

KEROSENE

Furnishing belt power for a John Deere Corn Sheller
—no gears in mesh at belt work.

CHAPTER 2

The Glory Years of the Two-Cylinders, 1918–1960

Above: *A farmer uses all his strength to spin the flywheel and start his Model D tractor. (Library of Congress)*

Left: *Waterloo Boy advertisement.*

Deere Waterloo Boy Models A, B, and C, 1918–1922

Following Deere's 1918 purchase of the Waterloo Gasoline Engine Company for $2.1 million, Deere management decided to continue building the Waterloo Boy Model N.

The recently purchased company had already been experimenting with an improved N. As they were exposed to dust and mud, the external final drives wore out quickly, so the first priority for a new model was to enclose the drive, but various solutions raised other problems. The first experimental model—known as the "bathtub" tractor—worked well, although the final-drive casing was too weak. Finally during the 1917–1918 winter, Waterloo Work's chief engineer, L. W. Witry, enclosed the roller chains in an oil bath, a system that lasted until 1953 on the subsequent Model D and was also a feature of the Model GP.

Seven Model A experimental tractors were built from 1919 to 1920 with the oil-bath final drive and bearing numbers 100–106. With permission from the Ford Motor Company, seven Model Bs, numbers 200–206, were built in 1921 using Fordson-style block-mounted front axles with necessary modifications. A final twelve Model Cs were built in 1922 and used all the improvements made in the first two batches, but retained the original Waterloo Boy 6.50x7.00-inch (162.5x175-mm) engine, now uprated to 800 rpm.

A 1920 Waterloo Boy Model N. Owners: Walter and Bruce Keller of Kaukauna, Wisconsin, USA. (Photograph © Andrew Morland)

Model D, 1923–1925

Despite the severe farm economy depression, Deere management decided to build a final Model D prototype in 1923. The Waterloo Boy N Series was approaching serial number 30400, so the new tractor became the Model D, number 30401, the first of the fourth style—and a new era was at hand.

The first 50 Model D tractors built in 1923 were distinguished by the ladder sides to the radiators and fabricated front axles. A further 829 tractors with 26-inch-diameter (65-cm) spoked flywheels were built in 1924.

Beginning with serial number 31280, shipped to California on October 8, 1924, the Model D was equipped with a 24-inch (60-cm) flywheel that was made thicker so it would weigh the same as the 26-inch (65-cm) flywheel it replaced. Also added were a jointed steering rod to keep the rod farther from the flywheel and a transmission case that would accept an external power takeoff (PTO) option.

For the balance of 1924 and all of 1925, the spoked flywheel was retained, the last example being shipped to the San Francisco branch on December 29, 1925. The first D with a solid flywheel left the works on January 2, 1926.

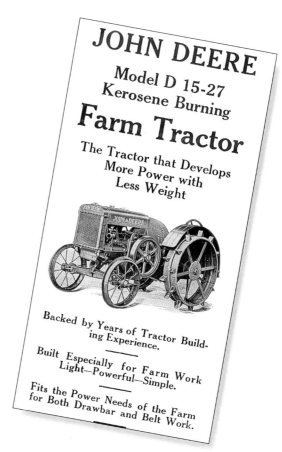

An original 1924 Model D brochure.

A 1924 spoke-flywheel Model D. (Photograph © Andrew Morland)

This 1924 Deere calendar image shows a youngster driving his Model D with a No. 5 plow and waving to an airplane and its pilot. The title of the image, "Aces All," tied together the farmer with the aviator of the 1920s, a hero of the period due largely to the exploits of Charles Lindbergh.

Above: *1924 spoke-flywheel Model D, number 31036. Owner: the Cobler family of Ottumwa, Iowa, USA.*

Right: *A detailed replica of the spoke-flywheel Model D in 1/16 scale constructed by farm toy custom builder Lyle Dingman of Spencer, Iowa, USA.*

Models D two-speed, DO, and D Crawler, 1926–1933

The two-speed Model D was introduced in 1926 and remained in production for nine years, but various improvements were made along the way. During 1927, the flywheel fitting to the crankshaft was changed from a key to six splines, and at the same time the engine bore was increased to 6.75 inches (168.75 mm), as it remained until 1953.

By 1928, a decision was made to upgrade the D, and in the fall, a batch of ninety-six experimental "Exhibit A" tractors was built with a three-speed gearbox, steel platform, improved fenders, enclosed PTO, and Model C–type right-hand steering. Although D production doubled in 1929, the Great Depression started that year in the United States and some of the proposed modifications had to be postponed.

Determined to continue with its search for improvements on the D, the company authorized a further batch of fifty experimental "Exhibit B" tractors, and these were built during summer 1930. The engine was beefed up, and its speed was increased from 800 to 900 rpm; both the steering and PTO position of the first Exhibit A batch were used.

By 1931, the agriculture market was improving, and from serial number 109944 most of the Exhibit A and B modifications were adopted, except the three-speed gearbox. The resulting increase in power was recorded by the University of Nebraska, with Test #236 showing 30.74 drawbar and 41.59 belt hp.

Following these experiments, other variations and prototype trials included the allocation of a total of ten machines for the addition of crawler half-tracks in place of the rear wheels; a few were supplied as Model DO orchard tractors, and three others were fitted with full tracks by the Lindeman Power Equipment firm of Yakima, Washington.

Below: *Two-speed Model D, number 68803. Owner: Derek Mellor of Peakdale, Derbyshire, England.*

Facing page: *Generations of farmers and farm equipment come together in this painting by artist Walter Haskell Hinton for Deere & Company.*

A 1927 advertisement retains the 15/27 description and has no reference to the Model D.

This 1927 brochure promotes the Deere 15/27 tractor, with no mention of the letter "D"!

A 1927 Model D. Owner: Frank Bettencourt, Vernalis, California, USA. (Photograph © Randy Leffingwell)

Models D three-speed and DI, 1934–1939

The final, unstyled version of the D appeared in late 1934 when the three-speed transmission was eventually adopted. By this time, rubber tires were increasingly used, and these required the adoption of the extra gear.

The D had been available for industrial use since 1925, but with the introduction of the third gear and its greater flexibility, the Model DI industrial was announced in 1935. Painted in highway yellow and with a higher-than-normal top speed of 7.5 mph (12 kph), it had low-pressure pneumatic tires as standard. The DI also featured a cushioned seat set at a right angle to the direction of travel; this required fitting extensions to the clutch lever, brake, and throttle controls. The DI continued in production until early1941, but was never styled. Only about one hundred Model DI tractors were built.

Above, top: *1936 Model DI, number 127198, with uphol-stered seat mounted at a right angle to the direction of travel. Owner: the Layher family, Wood River, Nebraska, USA.*

Above, bottom: *Model D, number 128492, alongside a Model BR, 332004. Owner: Jim Dance, Princes Risborough, Buckinghamshire, England.*

Left: *The 1937 brochure for the last unstyled Model D.*

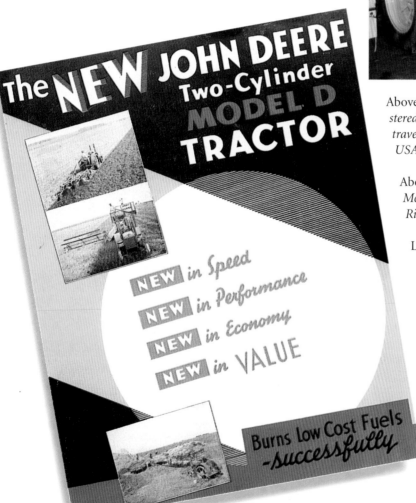

The NEW JOHN DEERE Two-Cylinder MODEL D TRACTOR

NEW in Speed
NEW in Performance
NEW in Economy
NEW in VALUE

Burns Low Cost Fuels –*successfully*

Model C, 1926–1927

With the success of the Model D assured, the company looked at the competition in the form of International Harvester's Farmall and decided there was a need for a smaller tractor that could serve this market and the row-crop farmer's requirements. Deere began experimenting in 1926 with five new tractors built in both three- and four-wheel form: The first to appear was a four-wheel, followed by two three-wheelers, and then two more four-wheels.

In 1927, Deere introduced the Model C, with a batch of twenty-four tractors numbered 101–122, 124, and 125; these were followed later in the year with seventy-five numbered between 200001 and 200110. Various teething troubles resulted in most of these initial models being recalled, reworked, renumbered, and reshipped. Of the original ninety-nine tractors, only fifty-three received new numbers; one is known to still exist, number 200109, owned by the Layhers in Nebraska, leaving the fate of the rest unknown.

The Model C was unique in being the first production tractor to offer the choice of four power outlets: belt pulley, drawbar, both front facing and rear PTO, and mechanical power lift.

Top: *This Model C, number 200109, is unusual as its serial number was not changed when the first batch of C tractors were returned to the factory for rebuilding as Model GPs. Owners: Walter and Bruce Keller of Kaukauna, Wisconsin, USA.*

Above: *The original 1929 Model C brochure.*

Left: *A Model C on display at the Two-Cylinder Club headquarters in Iowa. Owner: the Layher family, Wood River, Nebraska, USA.*

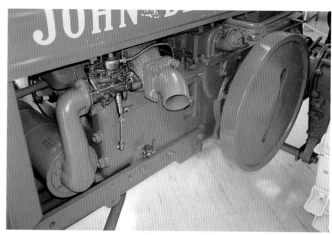

Above left: *The smooth-across rear-wheel hubs peculiar to the Model C.*

Above right: *Model C engine detail, including the straight-cut, round-end exhaust pipe, brass carburetor with water feed valve, and priming-cup decompression taps.*

Right: *This Ertl version of the Model C was a limited edition for a Two-Cylinder Club Expo.*

Model GP Series 1, 2, and 3, 1928–1935

In August 1928, the successor to the C was introduced as the Model GP, which was destined to remain in production in its various updated forms until February 1935. The first models were similar in appearance to the C, exceptions being the position of the front axle stops; a new-style seat support; the exhaust end, round on the C, oval on the GP; and the addition on the new model of "General Purpose" wording on the top of the hood.

Initially fitted with a similar 5.75x6.00-inch (143.75x150-mm) engine to the Model C, the first GP did not have vertical stacks; starting late in 1929, the air stack was routed through the hood. When the X/O, or "crossover," models were introduced in May 1930, they retained this feature. For the complete production of the smaller-engined models, the original cast oval main tank filler and threaded gas tank cap were retained.

Similar to the Model D tractors, all the 5.75-inch-bore (143.75-mm) tractors were equipped with water injection to the engine to prevent pre-detonation. With the change to the 6.00-inch (150-mm) bore on the X/O Model GP, water injection was eliminated.

Designed as a three-row tractor, the four-wheel arrangement of the GP was fine, but the requirement for either a two- or four-row model immediately became evident. This would soon lead to several variations of the Model GP.

Above right: *A 1930 Model GP brochure.*

Right: *1930 Model GP. Owner: Don Wolf of Indiana, USA. (Photograph © Andrew Morland)*

Above: *Right side of Model GP number 211860 showing the external vertical air cleaner of the second style of the GP. Model D 110570 stands behind. Owner: James Coward of Thorney, Cambridgeshire, England.*

Left: *An Ertl 1/16-scale model of the second style Model GP.*

Bottom left: *An Ertl 1/16-scale model of the third style Model GP with the air stack exit through the hood.*

Models GP X/O and GP Series 4 and 5, 1930–1935

In May 1930, the X/O "crossover" GP standards were introduced with 6.00-inch (150-mm) bore engines and no water injection system, although production of the smaller-bore tractors continued alongside the X/O. It was August before the change to the larger bore was completed on the standard models, starting with number 223803; at the same time, the air stack was moved to the left side, and the exhaust, complete with a new design of muffler and spark arrester with internal fins, to the right. This transformed the appearance of the tractor.

With the new models, several other updates were also fitted: Plain compression taps replaced the priming cups used previously, and a revised radiator core, radiator guard and curtain, crankcase breather and oil filter system were added as standard equipment.

The standard GP remained in production largely unchanged after this facelift from 1930 to 1935, although the option of 11.25x24-inch (28.125x60-mm) rubber tires from 1932 became increasingly popular. Other options available included a wider front axle to span two 28-inch (70-cm) rows of beets or edible beans. Another option was a lighting set with one front and one rear light powered by a generator.

Above: *A large-bore 1930 Model GP, number 224975, distinguishable by the vertical right-hand exhaust and left-hand air cleaner. Owner: Barry Bruce, Huntingdon, England.*

Right: *An Ertl 1/16-scale model of the last type of Model GP.*

Models GP Tricycle and side-steering GPWT, 1928–1932

From the beginning of the company's row-crop tractor development in 1926, the option of a tricycle layout was considered, with two of the first five experimental models being so equipped. Tricycle versions of the standard GP were included in the standard serial numbers in 1928 and through into 1929. In November 1928, the company decided to build fifty tricycles, but fourteen had already been built in August and September. Forty-nine came off the line between January 19 (number 202380) and February 13, 1929 (number 202428), and a further seven in March and April, resulting in seventy in all. Only two of the GP Tricycle models are known to exist at the time of this writing: numbers 204213, owned by the Kellers in Wisconsin, and 204072, found in Arizona by Allen and Charles Gould of Pierson, Michigan, in 1990, in time to be shown as found at Expo II.

The result of successful trials led to the production starting in late July 1929 of the newly designated Wide Tread, or GPWT. After the first few, a separate serial number sequence was chosen, starting with 400000; the earlier models with GP numbers were fitted in the field with new serial number plates. As with the standard models, the GPWTs first had the 5.75-inch-bore (143.75-mm) engine, then went through the 6.00-inch (150-mm) "crossover" stage, and finally had the 6.00-inch-bore engine with left-side vertical air stack and right-side muffler.

This Model GPWT, number 400047, was the forty-eighth built. The side-steer GPWT went through the same four styles as the standard model: no air cleaner stack or exhaust through the hood, air stack on the righthand side, air stack through the hood, and two vertical stacks. Owner: the Layhers family of Wood Green, Nebraska, USA.

The 1931 brochure for the side-steer Model GPWT.

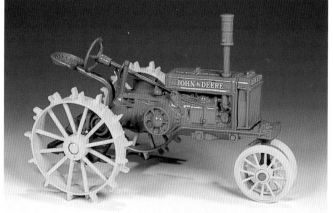

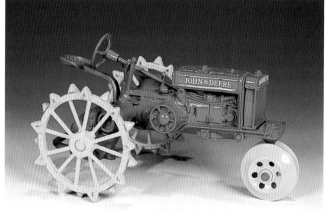

An Ertl 1/16-scale model of the third style of Model GPWT with the air stack through the hood.

An Ertl 1/16-scale model of the first style of Model GPWT.

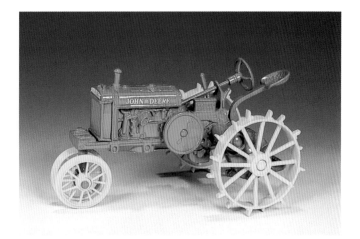

Model P, 1930–1931

In 1930, Deere produced a special "narrow wide-tread" GP variation tailor-made for the potato fields of Maine. At least two and possibly six of the last GP Tricycle models were built with this 68-inch-wide (170-cm) tread, and proved to be the forerunners of the P, or potato, Series. These were given separate serial numbers, from P 5000 to P 5202.

The first 150 were purpose built, but the last fifty-three were converted GP standard models re-numbered and with the original 5.75-inch (143.75-mm) bore, using up existing stock. Thus all the P tractors had the same engine with the through-the-hood air stack. Number P 5183, which had originally been GP number 222641, became experimental CX35 and was shipped to Argentina. It is thought to have been returned to Waterloo and rebuilt into P 5183.

The P was discontinued in 1931, and in its place a special pair of offset rear wheels was provided as an option for the normal GPWT to give the same 68-inch (170-cm) rear wheel tread.

Left, top: *The Ertl 1/16-scale Model P was the designated toy replica of the Two-Cylinder Club Expo V.*

Left, center: *Model P, number 5165, on round-spoke front and flat-spoke rear rubber wheels. Owner: the Cobler family, Ottumwa, Iowa, USA.*

Left, bottom: *Model P, number 5164, on steel wheels and complete with mid- and rear-mounted cultivators. Owner: the Cobler family, Ottumwa, Iowa, USA.*

Model GPWT over-head steering Style 5, 1932–1933

The final development of the GPWT Series arrived in 1932 with the introduction of over-hood steering beginning with number 404810.

Many improvements incorporated in this last series of GPWT tractors heralded the next and most important step in Deere row-crop design. The steering system was simplified by moving the steering rod above the hood and providing a front column ahead of the radiator; this in turn eliminated several joints. It also allowed the seating position to be raised and moved forward above the rear axle where an operator's platform was now provided. The seat was sprung and adjustable, and the throttle and spark controls were mounted on the steering wheel bracket ahead of the steering wheel, a more user-friendly arrangement. The frame was lengthened by 6 inches (15 cm), moving the radiator forward that distance and allowing the fuel tank and hood to be tapered to the rear, giving greatly improved visibility. Added to this was the inclusion of the muffler and air stack within the radiator/hood line.

Due to the depression of 1932–1933, only 445 of this model were built, making them the most prized wide-tread apart from the Tricycle and P models.

Left: *A restored over-hood-steer 1933 Model GPWT on rubber tires. The bail-type air stack and the retention of the earlier style's cast frame with holes for mid-mounted equipment are visible. This tractor is on round-spoke wheels all around.*

Bottom left: *The 1932 brochure shows both sides of the new Model GPWT on steel wheels.*

Below: *A 1932 brochure for the final style of Model GPWT.*

Model GPO, 1931–1935

Lindeman experimented in 1929 with a modification to a standard GP to lower it 7 inches (17.5 cm) for orchard work. The resulting tractor drew the attention of Deere personnel, and it was agreed that six experimental orchard tractors should be built in summer 1930. Taking GPWT crossover models with 6.00-inch (150-mm) bores from factory inventory, these six were converted by making a low front axle and reversing the rear axlehousing. The success of these tractors resulted in the introduction of production GPO tractors starting in February 1931 and continuing until April 1935. As with the P Series, a sepa-rate batch of serial numbers was allocated to these, start-ing at 15000.

Initially sold on steel wheels, a rubber-tire version was available from May 1932, and the Model GPO was shipped to all areas where orchards predominated—the West Coast, Michigan, and Florida figuring largely, although many also went to Canada.

More than 700 GPO tractors were built. Two of the most popular options were solid cast front wheels and full citrus fenders. A radiator guard and curtain were stan-dard equipment, as were low air stack and exhaust posi-tions outside the hood.

Crossover Model GPO, number 15223, on front cast wheels, an option for orchard work originally costing fifteen dollars. The extended air intake used on these particular models can be seen just beside the right fender. Owners: Walter and Bruce Keller of Kaukauna, Wisconsin, USA.

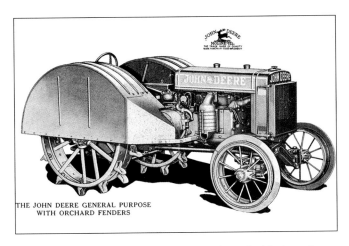

THE JOHN DEERE GENERAL PURPOSE
WITH ORCHARD FENDERS

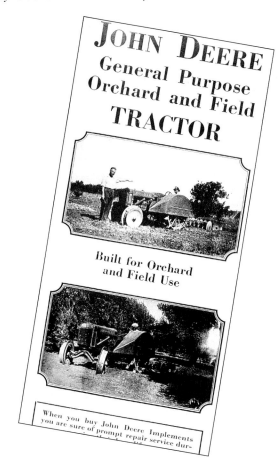

JOHN DEERE
General Purpose
Orchard and Field
TRACTOR

Built for Orchard
and Field Use

When you buy John Deere Implements
you are sure of prompt repair service dur–

Above: *The right-hand view of a GPO from the black-and-white 1932 brochure shows the orchard-type muffler.*

Right: *The same 1932 GPO brochure emphasised the low height of the tractor and the availability of cast front wheels and full citrus fenders.*

Model GPO-L, 1933–1934

The final model of the GP Series was an adaptation of the GPO, again by Lindeman in Yakima. Having established the orchard tractor idea with Deere, the next and last development of this series was to produce an orchard model on tracks. The GPO-L was fitted with four-roller track frames.

A few of the twenty-five or so GPO-L tractors have survived.

Model GPO-Lindeman, number 15703, has the horizontal air intake canister; others had a vertical air canister. Owner: John Nikodyn, Deere dealer of Red Cloud, Nebraska, USA.

Experimental Models FX, GX, AA-1, and AA-3; Model A, 1932–1934

Following the redesign of the GPWT, Deere engineers began thinking of its successor. In spring 1932, the experimental FX tractor was tested. This prototype was a modified over-hood-steer GPWT with several new trial features. It boasted the bail-type air stack and muffler in line to the left of the steering rod, spark plugs in the head, and a downward sweep to the cast-iron frame, which retained the front hole for toolbar attachment.

The GX appeared in fall 1932 and more closely resembled the production tractors that followed. One exception was that the water outlet ran from the head rather than the block.

In April 1933, eight AA tractors were built, six with four-speeds, known as the AA-1, and two three-speed AA-3s. The production of these latter ones was cancelled in June. A further four pre–Model A tractors, numbers 410008 through 410011, were built prior to full production, which started on March 19, 1934.

Seven of the first eight Model A tractors were recalled, rebuilt, and given new numbers. One, 410001, an AA-3, was scrapped. Of the next four, one kept its original number after rebuilding; three others were renumbered.

Up to number 414808, the A tractors had an open fan shaft and four-spoke steering wheel, and those to 459999 had ten-spline rear axles. The Model As all featured engines with a bore and stroke of 5.50x6.50 inches (137.5x162.5 mm) until 1940.

Right: *First of Ertl's 1/16-scale Precision Series, the unstyled Model A set a new standard in tractor modeling at a reasonable cost.*

A rear view taken from the 1933 Model A brochure illustrates Model AA features: bail-type air stack and no John Deere lettering on the rear axle housings.

Deere archival photograph of the experimental FX tractor in 1932. The similarities with the overhead-steer GPWT are obvious.

Above: *Two early Model A tractors, numbers 410008 and 410013. The former is a pre-production experimental model; the latter is the second production tractor.*

Right: *The first Model A brochure in December 1933 had an experimental Model AA on the cover with a four-spoke steering wheel.*

HARVEST TIME

—When dependable power equipment quickly pays for itself in time-, labor-, and crop-savings.

Deere archival photograph of a Model A on 1934-style Firestone tires with round-spoke wheels. The tractor is pulling a John Deere 5-A combine.

Top left: *The August 1935 forty-page brochure covers the Models A, AN, B, and BN, and much of the working equipment available for use with these tractors.*

Above: *An open-fanshaft Model A proclaims its age. It has the popular French & Hecht rear wheels made in Davenport, Iowa, across the Mississippi River from Moline.*

Left: *The second Precision Series replica from Ertl was the Model A, now on rubber tires with an integral cultivator painted red as on the original of the time.*

Models A, AN, AW, ANH, and AWH, 1935–1938

During 1935, a single-front-wheel version of the Model A, the AN, was announced, followed shortly by the AW with a wide-adjustable front axle, both models available on either steel wheels or rubber tires.

In 1937, the Hi-Crop ANH and AWH were added to the line with rubber tires only, and all were built after the change from ten- to twelve-spline rear axles at number 460000. These tractors offered greater clearance for bedded and other special crops. Their rear wheels had 40-inch (100-cm) centers in place of the standard 36 inches (90 cm).

Left: *Model AW. Owner: Don Wolf of Indiana, USA. (Photograph © Andrew Morland)*

Below: *The original September 1935 leaflet announcing the single-front-wheel versions, the AN and BN. The latter was also known as the Model B garden tractor.*

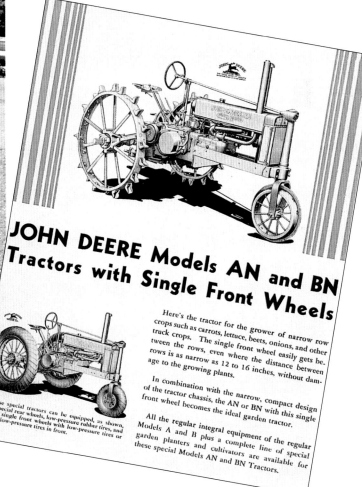

JOHN DEERE Models AN and BN Tractors with Single Front Wheels

Here's the tractor for the grower of narrow row crops such as carrots, lettuce, beets, onions, and other truck crops. The single front wheel easily gets between the rows, even where the distance between rows is as narrow as 12 to 16 inches, without damage to the growing plants.

In combination with the narrow, compact design of the tractor chassis, the AN or BN with this single front wheel becomes the ideal garden tractor.

All the regular integral equipment of the regular Models A and B plus a complete line of special garden planters and cultivators are available for these special Models AN and BN Tractors.

These special tractors can be equipped, as shown, with special rear wheels, low-pressure rubber tires, special single front wheels with low-pressure rubber tires, and double low-pressure tires in front.

Above: *Two unusual early high-crop models: unrestored Model AWH number 470232 and restored Model BWH number 57718. Owners: Walter and Bruce Keller of Kaukauna, Wisconsin, USA.*

Right: *Artist Walter Haskell Hinton captures the farm wife's call to the table in a painting that appeared in a classic John Deere calendar.*

Models AR, AO, and AI, 1935–1940

Both standard-tread and orchard versions of the A were introduced in 1935. When Deere decided to build the standard in January 1935, it originally referred to the model as the AS, or A standard; it was not until April that the tractors were finally referred to as the Model AR. The first AR tractors had offset radiator caps as on the unstyled A row-crop models; their numbers started at 250000.

The standard-tread Model AR holds a special place in my affection as the tractor that introduced me to John Deere. The unstyled, offset-radiator-capped AR with the later flat operator's platform has a lot to answer for. . . .

The first AO orchard model was built in May 1935, number 250075, and ended in October 1936, when the AOS was introduced. These early AO tractors were the same as the AR except they had independent rear wheel brakes, a low air stack, and a side-outlet muffler. The early AO tractors also had spoke front wheels.

Another version of this basic design was the AI industrial model. Production started in March 1936 and continued to June 1941. It varied from the AR with pads and tapped holes to the sides and front of the frame for attaching various types of industrial equipment, a 7-inch (175-mm) shorter wheelbase as on the AOS, heavy-duty drawbar, a strengthened rear axle, and a fixed cushion seat. One special AI, number 232346 owned by collector Don Dufner, has one-off electric starting and lighting and other unique features.

The October 1935 grove and orchard tractor brochure pictures the Model AO.

The December 1940 standard-tread field and orchard brochure shows the Model AR with an offset radiator cap and the Model AO with the new center-mounted cap.

Only 861 of the first Model AOs were built before the line was changed to the Model AOS streamline. This restored AO, number 251435, rides on full cast 24-inch (60-cm) rear wheels. Owner: Jack Bible of New Market, Tennessee, USA.

Left: *Model AR, number 259267.*

Below: *Model AI, number 252334, fitted with factory cab and sliding engine covers. Owner: the Layher family, Wood River, Nebraska, USA.*

Model AOS, 1936–1940

The streamlining added to the AOS, or AO streamlined, was a Deere innovation and not related to designer Henry Dreyfuss's influence. Development of the AOS began with six AR tractors that were rebuilt during 1936 as orchard models and given temporary numbers. These pre-AOS tractors were subsequently recalled: Two were scrapped and the other four were rebuilt and numbered in the AOS sequence. The experimental tractors were unique in having a dipstick for the oil level in place of the usual oil level cock.

To reduce the chance of damaging orchard trees, the AOS tractor was reduced in height, width, and length as compared to the AO it replaced. Still equipped with the original 5.50x6.50-inch (137.5x162.5-mm) engine, the front end support of the AI was used, reducing the wheelbase and thus the turning circle of the AOS. The overall height was reduced by 5 inches (125 mm) at the radiator cap, and the AOS was about 5 inches (125 mm) narrower. To obtain these dimensions, the width of the belt pulley was reduced, and the tractor was offset to take account of the remaining difference in width of the flywheel and pulley. A narrower front axle was also necessary.

The seating position was lowered, which meant that none of the wheels were visible from the seat, and the clutch lever was altered to give an up-and-down movement, a feature retained when the model was styled.

Special independent rear-wheel brakes were used, due to the confined space. The fenders were extended forward to the radiator, and optional citrus fenders were similarly extended to the same point. A redesigned radiator, cap, and pointed radiator guard were used to match the new styling. The tractor was offered on either steel wheels or with cast rears; fronts were round spoke.

Fewer than nine hundred AOS tractors were built: The AOS numbering started at 1000 in November 1936 and ended at 1891 in October 1940.

With so much design and engineering involved for so few tractors, Deere decided to return to the original AR/AO setup when the new, larger engine was adopted for the A Series, though with modifications. Thus, the unique AOS orchard tractors are eagerly sought after by collectors.

The only Model AOS in Great Britain, number 1432. Owner: Mrs. Towes of Cropthorne, Sussex, England.

Models AR and AO, 1941–1948

When the row-crop A was updated and fitted with the revised 5.50x6.75-inch (137.5x168.75-mm) engine in 1941, both the AR and AO were also updated. They had a central, pressed-steel round radiator cap from number 260000; they also had pressed-steel front wheels. The number of AOS and AI tractors built did not justify this change-over program, and they were discontinued.

Both the AR and AO were offered with electric starting and/or lighting options, options that were common in the models' later years. Another option was full citrus fenders for the orchard tractor. These last AO unstyled models had lowered steering and seat, and the low clutch lever engaged by pulling it up. Both the AO and AR continued in their unstyled form until 1949 and were the last models to be styled.

Top right: *Model AO. Owner: Patrick Looby of Johnstown, Kilkenny, Eire.*

Right: *The electric-start, center-radiator-cap Model AR with the unusual headlight position is beautifully reproduced here by custom builder Lyle Dingman.*

A large-engined, center-radiator-cap Model AR. The "AR" decal was only applicable for styled models, but was regularly supplied by Deere. The air stack has been foreshortened, and the rear tires are 14.9x26-inch (37.25x65-cm) oversize.

Experimental Model HX and Model B short frame, 1933–1935

In 1933, a model smaller than the A was envisaged, and the experimental HX was built, at least one of which had a bail-type air stack as used on the late GPWT and AA. A 16-hp tractor was the design objective: Deere plotted this model primarily for the small, row-crop farmer, but also as backup on larger farms. The engine measured 4.25x5.25 inches (106.25x131.25 mm), and ran at 1,150 rpm. No decompression taps were used, but a four-speed transmission was featured from the start. A PTO was to be standard equipment, and the choice of rubber tires was planned from the beginning.

The Model B followed the larger A in all respects, being about two-thirds its size in both weight and power. It was sold as a two-plow tractor with the work output of six to eight horses. Initially, the front pedestal was secured to the frame with four bolts, but this was soon changed, at number 3043, to eight. As with the A, the first few hundred tractors had center-line fuel tank filler caps, which were changed to the offset type to facilitate the use of a funnel. A Fairbanks-Morse magneto was used at first, but was soon replaced with a Wico. Similarly, a curtain with or without a radiator guard was offered to begin with, but shutters were an option from number 34952.

The eighth Model B built, number 1007, on round-spoke wheels.

Short-frame Model B, number 9161. The "Model B" decal is incorrectly placed on the hood instead of the seat channel. The skeleton wheels are obviously not designed for deep gravel. Note the casting cover over the rear brakes, as fitted on all these early Bs.

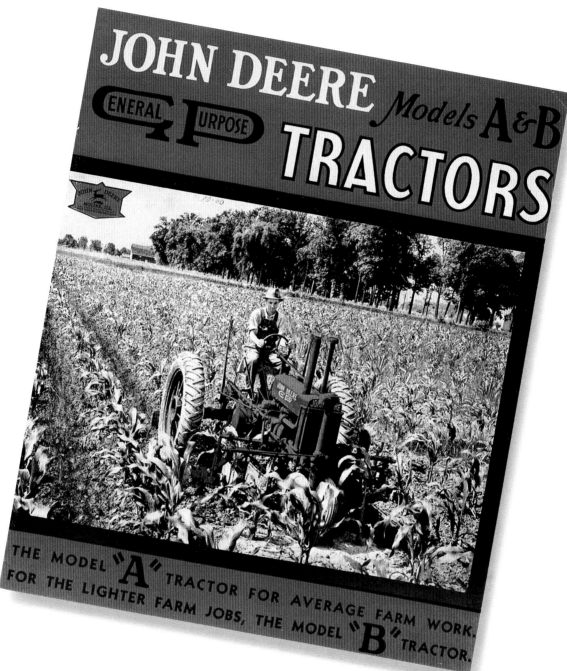

Above: *By the release of the October 1936 brochure covering the A and B Series, the line included the wide-front-axle Models AW and BW. The BW was available with both the original and a 5-inch-longer (125-mm) frame.*

Left: *Ertl's replica of the short-frame Model B.*

Above: *One of only twenty-four Model B garden tractors made, Model BN number 1798 has the early four-bolt pedestal fixing. Owners: Walter and Bruce Keller of Kaukauna, Wisconsin, USA.*

Models BN, BW, and BW-40 short frame, 1935–1937

Almost as soon as the production four-bolt B was marketed, a BN option was introduced and referred to in advertising literature as the B Garden Tractor. It was aimed at beet, lettuce, and vegetable growers, for crops grown in 28-inch-wide (70-cm) rows or less.

From February 1935, a third alternative to the basic B, the wide-front-axle BW, was offered, by which time the eight-bolt pedestal fixing was in use.

In 1936, six special wide-front-axle models were built with narrower axles, and these are now called the BW-40.

Below: *1935 Model BN. Owner: Bob Pollock of Denison, Iowa, USA. (Photograph © Randy Leffingwell)*

Above: *A restored early Model BW with a standard wide front axle, old-style fenders, and round-spoke wheels front and rear.*

Left: *Model BW-40 with Kay Brunner aftermarket cast steel rear wheels. Note the wide-front with extensions. Owner: Robert Lovegrove of Fairmont, Nebraska, USA.*

Bottom left: *Model BW replica on rubber tires.*

Model B long frame, 1937–1938

One problem arose when the unstyled A and the first B were used on the same farm: The mid-mounted toolbars were not interchangeable. To resolve this, the frame of the B was extended 5 inches (125 mm) to be the same length as the A. The change took place during 1937, starting at number 42200, and involved a number of alterations to the hood, fuel tank, fan and steering shafts, and water and exhaust pipes. Along with these changes, the loop drawbar was replaced with the regular type.

There were far fewer long-frame unstyled B tractors built than the original short version, so, like the four-speed styled models of both the A and B, they are of more interest to collectors.

Model B, number 52234, showing the slightly staggered air stack of the unstyled Bs. The long-frame tractor retained the cast cover over the rear brakes. Owner: David Lee of Norfolk, England.

Models BN, BNH, BW, BW-40, BWH, and BWH-40, 1937–1938

In addition to the BN and BW variations, Deere fitted some BN tractors in fall 1937 with larger, 16-inch (40-cm) front wheels and rubber tires, and 40-inch (100-cm) rears instead of the standard 36-inch (90-cm) to give them greater clearance. The result was the BNH Hi-Crop.

In 1936, six BW models were shipped with special narrow front axles—parts from the BR and BO—to reduce the tractor's width and a narrow rear axle, creating the rare BW-40.

By December 1937, certain BWs were also adapted for high crops, creating the BWH. When provided with narrow front and rear axles, a fourth and final row-crop version of the BW was produced, the BWH-40.

Model BW, number 53506. Note the road bands on both the front and rear wheels. Owner: Chris Goodley of Outwell, Cambridge, England.

Above, top: *An Ertl replica of the Model BR on rubber tires.*

Above, bottom: *Two restored Model BRs, number 328016 in front, 328011 behind. Both are on all-round-spoke wheels. Owner Scott McAllister of Mt. Pleasant, Iowa, USA.*

Experimental Model HX-83 and Model BR, 1935–1947

As with the A, a standard model of the B Series was needed, and in summer 1935, the HX-83 experimental predecessor of the BR was produced. Like the row-crop models, the small-engined tractors had no decompression taps. In 1939, the engine was increased in size to 4.50x5.50 inches (112.5x137.5 mm), and compression taps were a necessary fitting.

From the beginning, the BR had optional steel wheels or rubber tires. The former were round-spoke 5.00x24 inches (12.5x60 cm) on the front and flat-spoke 8.00x40-inch (20x100-cm) rears. Rubbers were round-spoke, 5.50x16-inch (13.75x40-cm) front and the choice of 11.25x24-inch (28x60-mm) or 9.00/10.00x28-inch (22.5/25x70-mm) cast rears. An 11.25x24-inch (28x60-mm) round-spoke rear was also offered. From 1942, the rears were changed to 11.00x26 inches (27.5x65 mm), and these were used to the end of production in 1947. Steel fronts with rubber rears or rubber fronts with steel rears could also be ordered.

During 1937, a radiator shutter replaced the original guard and curtain. In September 1939, a new option was electric starting and lighting. The large 7-inch (17.5-cm) lamps, as used on the Model D option, were supplied. This was one of the last changes made to these sought-after and handy little tractors.

A 1935 Model BR. (Photograph © Andrew Morland)

Small-engined Model BO, number 328087. Owner: Brian Davey of Norfolk, England.

Electric-start late Model BO, number 337420. These late tractors had 26-inch (65-cm) rear tires.

Ertl's Model BO replica is complete with full citrus fenders.

Model BI, number 326025, with the armchair seat fitted on all industrial models of this era. This BI rides on 28-inch (70-cm) rear wheels; an optional size on early Models BR, BO, and BI was 24 inches (60 cm). Owner: the Layher family, Wood River, Nebraska, USA.

Models BO and BI, 1935–1947

Specifications and options for the BR also applied to the BO orchard and BI industrial. In addition, the BO was equipped as standard with differential turning brakes, air intake through the hood, and shielded fuel filler caps; citrus fenders were optional. Apart from these changes, the BO and BR were identical and were in the same serial number sequence. The first BO was the eighty-fifth number allocated, and the last model was eight numbers before the end of production.

The BI was also numbered with the BR, with the first experimental BI being 325617, from February 1936. Due to lack of demand, however, the BI was cancelled at the end of February 1941, after only 181 were built. They were painted highway yellow with black lettering.

As on the AI, the front of the BI frame had pads with tapped holes added for fixing industrial equipment; for the same reason, the front axle was moved back 5.25 inches (131.25 mm) to keep these front-mounted units nearer the radiator, as well as giving a shorter turning radius. Other features included a heavier, shorter drawbar; stronger back axle; rigidly mounted cushion seat; air stack like the BR but shorter; and the option of rear wheel brakes. The limited number built increases their desirability to collectors.

Model BO-L, 1943–1946

Nearly seventeen hundred BO crawlers were built by Lindeman, most of them from BO tractors supplied without wheels by Deere. Some BR tractors made up the shipment, and one BI was sent, number 330986. This particular unit was supplied because of the possibility of a military contract, which did not materialize. The BO-L was popular in the northwestern states.

On January 1, 1947, the Lindeman plant became part of the John Deere empire.

Right: An original Lindeman leaflet detailing the firm's crawler conversion for the Model BO.

Below: *A 1945 Model BO-L. (Photograph © Andrew Morland)*

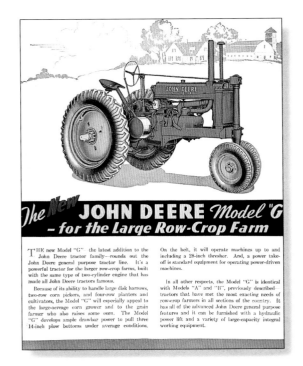

THE new Model "G" the latest addition to the John Deere tractor family—rounds out the John Deere general purpose tractor line. It's a powerful tractor for the larger row-crop farms, built with the same type of two-cylinder engine that has made all John Deere tractors famous.

Because of its ability to handle large disk harrows, two-row corn pickers, and four-row planters and cultivators, the Model "G" will especially appeal to the large-acreage corn grower and to the grain farmer who also raises some corn. The Model "G" develops ample drawbar power to pull three 14-inch plow bottoms under average conditions.

On the belt, it will operate machines up to and including a 28-inch thresher. And, a power take-off is standard equipment for operating power-driven machines.

In all other respects, the Model "G" is identical with Models "A" and "B", previously described tractors that have met the most exacting needs of row-crop farmers in all sections of the country. It has all of the advanced John Deere general purpose features and it can be furnished with a hydraulic power lift and a variety of large-capacity integral working equipment.

Details of the Model G in its original form with the small radiator, from the February 1938 brochure. Note the gap between the steering rod and its top tank.

Electric-start Model BO-L, number 336427. Electric starting was one of the later options on all BR, BO and BO-L tractors.

Experimental Model KX and Model G, 1935–1941

Following the introduction of the Models A and B, it soon became obvious that farmers required a row-crop tractor that was more powerful than the A, and the KX experimental tractors were designed and in the field by 1935. Having already used A, B, C, and D for tractor models and E for the stationary engines, the new model was to be called the F. International Harvester already had its Farmalls in production with the "F" prefix for the F-20 and the rest of the line, so Deere decided to name the new tractor the Model G so it would not be confused with the competition. This explains the "F" prefix for all Model G parts.

Advertised as a full three-plow tractor, the new model had a larger, 6.125x7.00-inch (153.125x175-mm) engine, governed at the same 975 rpm as the A. The larger engine necessitated a curve in the chassis frame to accommodate the extra engine width; this feature remained with this size model through to the end of two-cylinder production. The first tractors soon had problems with overheating, so from number 4250, a larger radiator was fitted; at the same time, a new hood, fuel tank, and other parts were added.

All G tractors had a shift quadrant and a single lever for the four-speed gearbox, unlike the smaller models. Available on steel or rubber tires, the latter soon became the more popular. The unstyled models were never offered with a single front wheel or wide axle.

The first unstyled G was built in May 1937 and the last in December 1941.

A beautiful 1/16-scale replica of the Model BO–Lindeman crafted by custom builder Gilson Riecke of Ruthven, Iowa, USA.

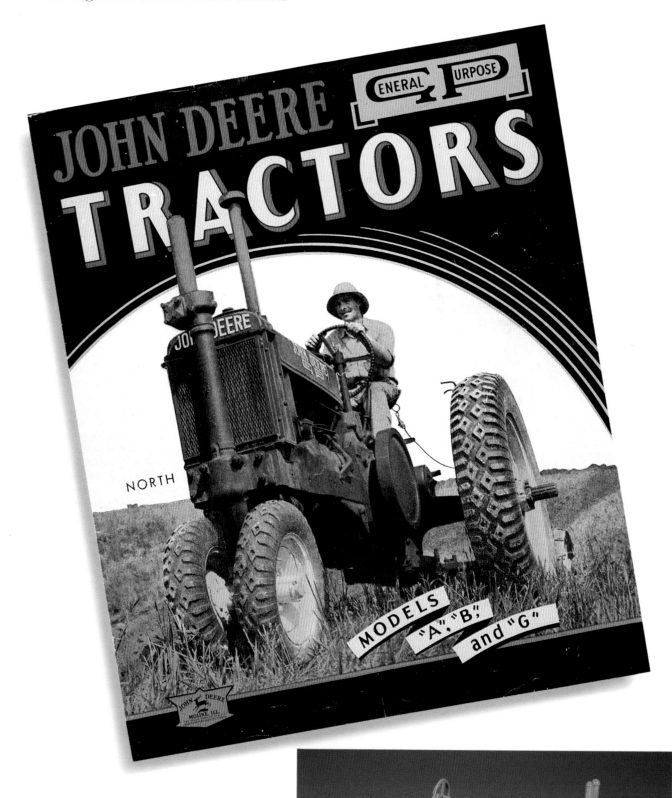

Above: *The A-188-2-38 General Purpose Tractors brochure added the Model G to the A and B for the first time.*

Right: *The standard 1/16-scale Ertl replica of the unstyled Model G.*

A replica of the Model Y, complete with Novo engine, built by Jack Kreeger from original Deere drawings. Kreeger, of Omaha, Nebraska, specializes in all things to do with the L Series and its beginnings.

Unstyled Model L, number 622341. This was the second L purchased by the author. Owner: Bill Kemball of Wantisden, Suffolk, England.

Models Y, 62, and L, 1935–1938

Deere's smallest pre–World War II tractor line was developed in the old Moline wagon works in 1935. Management's instruction was to develop a small tractor—but not to spend any money at it! In 1936, the Model Y was announced, powered by a Novo two-cylinder vertical gas engine, followed later by a Hercules. The transmission and steering were from Ford Model A cars. Twenty-four were built, but all were probably scrapped.

By 1937, the lessons learned from the Y were applied to a new series, the Model 62. Seventy-nine of these, numbered 62.1000 to 62.1078, were built between January and July 1937.

In August 1937, the Model 62 became the unstyled L, starting at number 62.1079. The 62 is easily distinguished from the L as it has a large "JD" logo on the casting below the radiator and on the rear axle banjo. The cast rear wheels of the 62 were also a different style, and the fenders extended further over them. These models introduced the idea of an offset engine position to improve visibility while in row crops.

Records of the number of 62 and unstyled L tractors have been lost and are therefore a matter of conjecture. The last serial number has been variously put at 62.2563 and 62.2580, a total production of around fifteen hundred. As a result of the small numbers built, the 62 is collectible, and the unstyled L commands ever-increasing prices.

Below: *Model 62, number 1039. Note the "JD" on the casting below its radiator. Owners: Annette and Mike Bellin of Isanti, Minnesota, USA.*

Lanz Gross-Bulldog HR2, HR4, HR5, and HR6, 1926–1935

The line of tractors from Lanz, which finally became Deere's European arm in 1956, took a giant step forward in 1926 with the introduction of the Model HR2 22/28-hp Gross-Bulldog. These tractors were still single-cylinder diesels equipped with hopper cooling, but represented a considerable advance on the original Bulldog design.

The Model HR2 was further improved in 1929 with radiator instead of hopper cooling, becoming the Model HR4. Radiator-cooled Bulldogs, from a small 13-hp model to the large 60-hp types, would continue to appeared in many versions between 1932 and 1960.

The new HR4 had the added advantage of a gearbox with three forward and one reverse speeds; the practice until then had been to reverse the direction of travel of the early Bulldog motors.

Introduced with an engine speed of 540 rpm, these standard-tread tractors were Europe's contemporary model to the two-speed, all-fuel Deere D. The plowing version had speeds of 2 to 5 mph (3.2-8 kph), while a solid rubber-tired road option gave 3 to 9 mph (4.8-14.4 kph).

Above: An advertisement featuring the latest Bulldog for the July 1929 Royal Show in England.

Below: A HR2 brochure shows the steel-wheeled field tractor with angled grousers and a number of its farming uses.

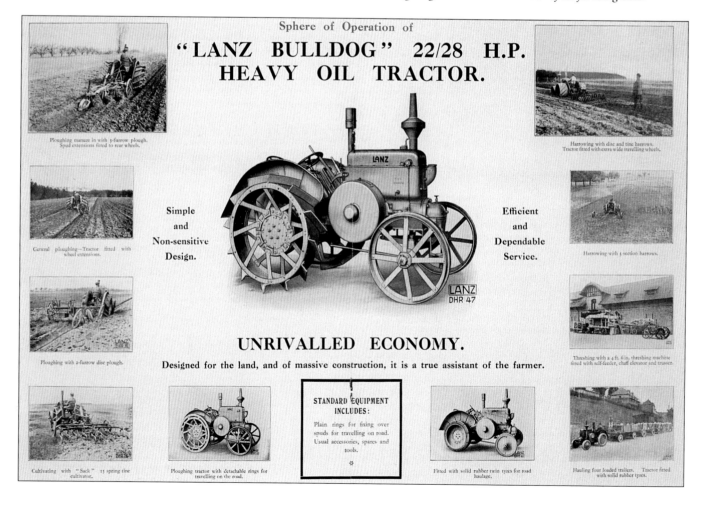

It was not until the introduction of the radiator-cooled, 30-hp 15/30 HR5 and 38-hp HR6 that sales really took off. These new models had a right-hand, V-belt drive from the crankshaft to the fan shaft; the fan was between the two radiator cores. Learning of the trials in the United States using rubber tires supplied by Firestone, Lanz contacted Continental of Hannover, Germany, and after successful tests, the HR5 was offered on rubber tires in 1929. With a modified governor it was possible to increase the engine revs to 630 rpm, giving a higher road speed.

Tested in 1930 by Oxford University in England, the current Bulldog was pitted against ten gas, eleven kerosene, and five diesel tractors from competing makers. Tests included brake power ratings at half, three-quarters, and full power, and an eight-hour drawbar and maximum drawbar pulling test. In all of them, the Lanz was the most economical to operate, the judges taking fuel, lubricating oil, and water consumption into account. The relative purchase price was also low.

Starting in 1926, Lanz offered add-on half-track conversions for the Bulldogs, but it was 1935 before full crawler tractors were put into production. Four prototype crawlers were built in 1933 and twenty-one pre-production machines were constructed in 1934.

The HR5 and HR6 remained in production until 1935.

Why I am the Champion of my Class

Lanz Bulldog
Crude Oil Tractor

Right, top: *The HR2 22/28-hp road tractor with hopper cooling and twin solid rears. The tractor was on display in the Mannheim Works Museum, Germany.*

Right: *Brochure for the HR4 and HR5 radiator-cooled Bulldogs.*

Lanz Bulldog 12/20 HN1 and HN2, HN3 (D-7500), HN4, HR7 (D-8500), HR8 (D-9500), and HR9 (D-1500), 1931–1955

As with Deere's Model GP, created as a smaller sibling of the D, a smaller version of the radiator-cooled Bulldog was needed for smaller farms. This resulted in the 12/20 HN1 of 1931–1934 and a less-expensive version, the HN2 of 1934–1935. In both models, the fan drive was moved to the left side, and a six-speed gearbox was optional with rubber tires.

In 1931, Lanz used a Deere GPWT as a model for a row-crop version of the HN1, but the demand for this type was not sufficient in Europe to justify production.

The HN2 replacement, the 20-hp HN3, was announced in 1935 and remained in production until 1952, except for the war years when tractor production ceased because allied bombers virtually destroyed the Mannheim works.

With the HN3 Bulldog, a new style of model designation was introduced, the D Series. The first examples were the 25-hp D-7500, 35-hp D-8500, and 45-hp D-9500.

Only six examples of the HN4 were built in 1936, and they were the 25-hp prototype for the HN3 when it was uprated to 25-hp. All these later HN3/HN4 models were sold as D-7500 Series tractors.

Within the D series, the D-7500 was a basic, steel-wheeled tractor; the D-7501 had starting ignition and lighting; the D-7502 had only the lighting; the D-7506 had rubber tires and six-speed gearbox. This method of numbering remained in effect into the years of Deere ownership and through to the end of the Bulldog era.

Pre-war production amounted to more than 25,000 of the HN1 to HN4 12/20 hp series from 1932 to 1941; and more than 40,000 of the HR Series from the HR4 to HR9.

Below: *35-hp HR7. This was also known as the D-8506 under the new Lanz numbering system. Owner: Peter Parfitt, Cambridgeshire, England.*

Above, bottom: *45-hp D-9506, number 133295. It makes an interesting comparison with the British Field Marshal next to it. Owner: A. Baker of Hailsham, Sussex, England.*

Lanz Bulldog D-4500, D-5500, D-9500, D-1500, D-3500, D-7500, and D-8500; export Bulldog Models JL, N, and P, 1935–1952

A larger Bulldog was soon needed in addition to the smaller models, so in 1936, the existing models were uprated. The 30-hp 540-rpm D-8500 Series became 35 hp; the 38-hp 630-rpm D-9500 Series became 45 hp; and a new 55-hp 750-rpm model was announced, the D-1500 Series.

In some markets, the various models had single-letter classifications: For example, the D-7506 was called the J and the D-3506 the L.

For 1940 only, a smaller, 15-hp Bulldog was offered, the D-4506. Only 276 were built.

Below: *This Eil, or "Speedy," Bulldog was built in 1939, and powered by a large 629-ci (10.3-liter) engine. These Bulldog road models had five or six forward gears that could be changed on the move and a top speed of 25 miles per hour (40 km/h). Open and closed cabin versions of the Eil Bulldog were offered with or without winches. Owner: Pierre Bouillé of France. (Photograph © Andrew Morland)*

Below: *This 1950 Lanz Bulldog D-7506 was fitted with pneumatic tires, which were called* Ackerluft, *literally "field air." The D-7506 Bulldog was rated at 25 horsepower. Owner: Jim Thomas of Wokingham, England. (Photograph © Andrew Morland)*

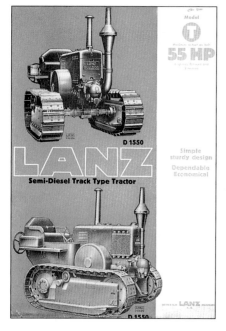

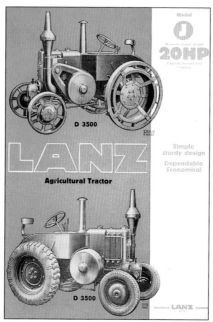

Above: This 1951 Lanz Bulldog D-9506 had a 45-horsepower hot-bulb engine of a massive 629-ci (10.3-liter) displacement. Owner: Daniel Binet of Normandy, France. (Photograph © Andrew Morland)

Far left: The 55-hp D-1550 crawler version of the D-1506 wheeled tractor.

Left: An early leaflet for the D-3500 three-speed 20-hp agricultural Model J.

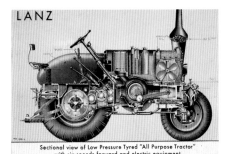

Sectional view of Low Pressure Tyred "All Purpose Tractor" with six speeds forward and electric equipment

Right, top: *Export model 45-hp D-9516, number 650680. Owner: Tony Fisher, England.*

Above: *Cross-section drawing of the HR8 or D-9500 Series.*

Right: *A comprehensive Lanz export brochure covering the D Series from the 16-hp D-5506 to the 45-hp D-9506. Apart from the D-5506, which was not introduced until 1950, the rest were in the line from 1936 to 1952.*

CHAPTER 3

The Styled Years, 1938–1955

Above: *A trio of salesman show off the new, styled Deere Model A with the Roll-O-Matic front end at the Minnesota State Fair in the 1940s. (Minnesota State Fair collection)*

Left: *Picture perfect: The farmer's daughter snaps a photograph of the farm's prized bull and Deere tractor in this painting by Walter Haskell Hinton.*

Model D, 1939–1953

Although the D was the third series of Deere tractors, after the Models A and B, to be styled by Henry Dreyfuss, it was still the premier model in the pre–World War II Deere tractor line. The styled D holds my affection since serial number 154757 was the first Deere tractor I owned, purchased new on February 8, 1943. My styled D was on steel wheels, the only wartime option available, and it proved to be excellent both in running a belt-powered thresher and in plowing with an International 8C four-bottom plow; together, we plowed more than 450 acres (180 hectares) in the first year.

The earlier styled Model D had round-spoke front wheels and 28-inch (70-cm) rears, but from number 150617, the fronts became the disk type and the rears were changed to 30 inches (75 cm). The auxiliary air cleaner was a straight cylindrical type to begin with, but the later models adopted a mushroomlike top. Due to the size of the engine, a popular option on later models was electric starting, available with or without lighting. Another, and even more popular, option was the provision of a PTO, available since the late 1920s. One rare option was rear wheel brakes, which could be operated separately with foot pedals for shorter turns, or together with a hand-operated lever. Various lugs, grousers, and extension rims were available for steel-wheeled models, as well as different-size sprockets for faster speeds.

The Model D was in production longer than any other tractor built by Deere or the competition. It survived for thirty-one years, from 1923 to 1953. Such was its popularity that after production had officially ceased in 1952, an extra batch had to be built by popular demand; these tractors were assembled in the street between the millroom and truck shop at Waterloo, and thus became known as "Streeters." A truly great tractor, the D has an exhaust sound all its own.

The 1939 Model D brochure.

Styled Model D, number 172641, unusually fitted with electric lights but not electric starting. Owner: Wout Veldman of Zuidwolde, The Netherlands.

Above: *The steel-wheel version of the styled Model D.*

Right: *Deere's five standard-model agricultural tractors available in 1940: the D, AR, AO, BR, and BO.*

The June 1938 sales brochure unveiled the first photographs of the new styled A and B on rubber tires.

The June 1938 brochure for the new styled Models A and B.

Model A, AN, AW, ANH, and AWH four-speed, 1938–1940

The first two models styled by industrial designer Henry Dreyfuss were the row-crop Models A and B. Other makes—Oliver in particular—had led the way with styling, so Deere decided in 1938 to adopt styling for all applicable machines—tractors, combines, and other harvesters, to name a few. Deere chose Dreyfuss's New York firm, their theme was adopted, and a family likeness was created.

In its first styled form, starting with number 477000, the Model A had a four-speed gearbox. Apart from the styling, the tractors were mechanically similar to the unstyled models.

From number 488000, the A Series was given a larger engine, the stroke being increased from 6.50 to 6.75 inches (162.5 to 168.75 mm). In Nebraska tests, this showed an increase in power from 18.72 to 26.20 drawbar and 24.71 to 29.59 belt hp. The four-speeds also had a 1⅜-inch (34.375-mm) PTO in place of the 1⅛-inch (28.125-mm) of the earlier models; the main transmission case was strengthened; and fifteen-spline rear axles replaced the twelve-spline.

For the first time in the company's history, electric starting was offered as an extra. To accommodate the battery behind the fuel tank, the hood was extended and a slanted dash was used with the gauges and steering support incorporated.

In addition to the twin-front-wheel A, variations included the single-front AN, wide-front axle AW, and the AWH and ANH. These Hi-Crop models had larger-diameter wheels: 16-inch (40-cm) fronts replacing the 10-inch (25-cm) in the N Series, and 40-inch (100-cm) rears in place of the 36-inch (90-cm) standard wheels on both series, with longer front spindles on the W Series.

The four-speed models remained in production for just over two years.

Model AN four-speed, number 478570. Note the local road plates and license disc holder, round-spoke rear wheels, and optional fenders. Owner: M. Watson, Long Sutton, Lincolnshire, England.

Model A, AN, AW, ANH, and AWH six-speed, 1940–1946

In September 1940, the A models were given a six-speed transmission with a gate change instead of the earlier gear stick straight from the gearbox. At the same time, rear wheels were changed to 38 inches (95 cm) and decals with black edging replaced the previous silk screening. Due to lack of certain materials during wartime, tractors from 523600 to 542699 were fitted with pressure radiators, but returned to the standard type thereafter. Options included fenders, hydraulic Power Lift, various alternative wheel equipment, and in 1945, Power-Trol, allowing accurate positioning of the rockshaft and use of an external cylinder. All these updates brought the A back into the largest-selling category it previously enjoyed and lifted it into the three-plow category in lighter soils.

Above: *1942 six-speed Model A with a No. 5 mower attached. Owner: Wout Veldman of Zuidwolde, The Netherlands.*

The 1/16-scale Ertl replica of the six-speed Model A fitted with a long hood to accommodate the battery for the electic starting and lighting option.

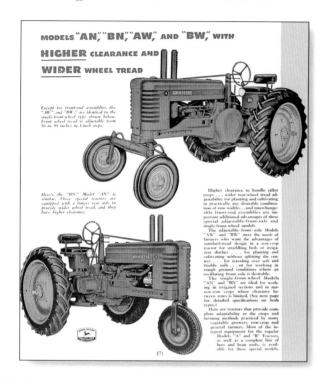

Model A, AN, AW, and AH six-speed electric, 1947–1952

Early in 1947, the A received another upgrade as electric starting and lights became standard. The new frames were pressed steel, and the seat was now an armchair type with the battery moved into a box beneath. At the same time, the starter was moved to its own compartment in the bottom of the main case, allowing the flywheel to be enclosed. The steering column was modernized with both the throttle and shutter levers included in the design.

Serial numbers of the new models started at 584000, but the most significant change was the option of gas-only as well as all-fuel engines. With the extra power generated by these gas engines, 34.14 drawbar and 38.02 belt hp was achieved at Nebraska; thus the A was now a full three-plow tractor in most soils. With the demand for increased power, the A returned to the favorite spot with farmers.

The ANH and AWH were dropped, and the AN and AW were offered with either 38- or 42-inch (95- or 105-cm) rear wheels and balancing fronts. The front columns on these models were split and held with four bolts, so that they became interchangeable. A split column for the A was another option, as was the Roll-O-Matic knee-action twin-front wheel.

One more change was to come at number 648000: The B had single-stick gear control, so the A was similarly equipped. A host of other detail changes occurred in the last years of production: Square rear axlehousing, clamshell fenders, distributor ignition, larger fuel tank, and black-face gauges were all added. Finally in 1950, the AH Hi-Crop was announced, with many parts interchangeable with the GH.

Left, top: *The late-style, electric-start gas Model AW and BN all-fuel as illustrated in the 1951 sales brochure.*

Left, center: *Six-speed Model AN, number 550301, complete with fenders.*

Left, bottom: *"Pint-Sized Shadow," a painting by artist Walter Haskell Hinton showed Junior at work with his Deere toy while Dad greased the front end of the Real McCoy. (Deere & Company)*

The May 1947 brochure covered both updated Model A and B tractors.

Top: *V for victory: While the men go off to fight in World War II, this woman takes over the Deere in this 1945 painting by artist Walter Haskell Hinton for Deere & Company.*

Above: *Ertl's Model A is based on the gasoline version with a single fuel tank.*

Model B, BN, BW, BNH, BWH, and BWH-40 four- and six-speed, 1938–1946

The B was the model used for styling experiments, but both the restyled A and B were announced to the public at the same time. In the case of the B, the opportunity was taken to increase its power by adding an extra 0.25 inches (6.25 mm) to both bore and stroke. This increased power on steels from 11.84 to 14.03 drawbar hp, and 16.01 to 18.53 belt hp or 16.44 drawbar hp on rubber tires.

Twelve-spline rear axles, as fitted to the unstyled BNH and BWH, replaced the ten-spline of the earlier models, and the whole back end was strengthened. As with its larger sibling, in 1940 the B Series was offered with electric starting and lighting and the resulting long hood. It was also changed from 36- to 38-inch (90- to 95-cm) rear wheels.

The 1941 model had an extension to its muffler, and rubber-tired versions received a six-speed transmission like the A. Again, material shortages during the war made the fitting of pressure radiators necessary from numbers 148500 to 166999. The PTO on the B was increased to 1⅜ inches (84.375 mm) from number 149700 to remain in line with the competition, but war conditions precluded any further changes.

The styled B was available as a twin-front B, single-front BN, normal wide-axle BW, BNH and BWH Hi-Crops, and a special BWH-40 with 42-inch (105-cm) rear tread for 40-inch (100-cm) bed crops; only twelve BWH-40 tractors were built. As on the unstyled models, the rear tires were originally 36 inches (90 cm) on standard models and 40 inches (100 cm) on the Hi-Crops, all of which were rubber tired. Power-Trol was an option from October 1945.

Left: *Model BWH-40, number 94438. All but one of the twelve BWH-40s were originally shipped to California. Owners: Walter and Bruce Keller of Kaukauna, Wisconsin, USA.*

Above: *Dad jumps off his trusty Deere to help Junior, who has snagged a turtle at the old fishing hole in this painting by artist Walter Haskell Hinton for Deere & Company.*

This 1/16-scale Ertl Model B has the long hood and electric starting.

A restored Model BW, which even includes the silk-screened "Made in USA" under the "John Deere" decal, which was normal practice on export models. Owner: John Turner of Grafton, Hampshire, England.

Model B, BN, and BW electric, 1947–1952

The B was introduced in 1947 with all the same alterations announced for the A: pressed-steel frame, electric starting and lights standard, the battery moved under the cushioned seat, modern steering column, and a four-stud split-front column option after number 259371.

Most significant with the B Series was the increase in engine size and power. The bore was enlarged from 4.50 to 4.6875 inches (112.5 to 117.1875 mm) and the rated

speed from 1,150 to 1,250 rpm at full load. The resulting power figures at Nebraska were 24.62 drawbar and 27.58 belt hp for the gas models and 21.14 drawbar and 23.53 belt hp for the all-fuel, a 15 percent increase in the latter case.

The new models started at number 201000 in February 1947. To allow for the cancellation of the BNH and BWH, which never sold in great numbers, the BN and BW were offered with the choice of 38- or 42-inch (95- or 105-cm) rear wheels and equivalent fronts. All other options followed the Model A.

1952 Model BN, number 295281. Owner: Royce Lambert of San Luis Obispo, California, USA.

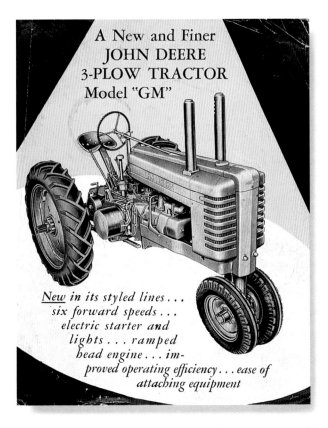

*New in its styled lines . . .
six forward speeds . . .
electric starter and
lights . . . ramped
head engine . . . im-
proved operating efficiency . . . ease of
attaching equipment*

The April 1941 leaflet describing the new six-speed Model GM styled tractor.

Experimental Model GX and Model GM, 1942–1947

With the new styling of the A, B, and D, the G was the next in line. During 1941, four GX experimental models were tested, and in early 1942, the new tractors went into production. To remain in line with the smaller models, the new tractors had a six-speed transmission, which involved a redesign of the gear case, and the introduction of a hi-lo lever, although a cast main-gear-lever quadrant was retained. Electric starting and lighting were optional, and they were the external type fitted on top of the main case as used on the D.

With these extensive modifications, a price rise was obviously needed, but, with new wartime government restrictions in force, this was refused. To overcome this, the model designation was changed to GM, or G modernized. Despite this, the serial number plates carried the Model GM stamp but still had G-13XXX numbers.

Production of the GM initially lasted only eight months when wartime restrictions forced its temporary cessation for two years; the line was started again in October 1944, and continued until March 1947. The last GM built was number 22112.

Model GM, number 18742. The battery position on these tractors, pan seat, and external-type electric-starting option are all visible. The six-speed gearbox operation was achieved with a Hi-Lo lever as on earlier A and B versions. Owner: James Coward of Thorney, Cambridgeshire, England.

Models G, GN, GW, and GH, 1947–1953

On March 7, 1947, the G Series was revived with serial number 23000, still equipped with the pan seat and forward battery location for electric-start models. The G also had the Roll-O-Matic option of the smaller models, and the split-front pedestal, allowing the introduction of the GN and GW models.

This new G Series only lasted until July 1947, when the model was given the armchair seat with the battery beneath, and electric starting and lighting as standard. Again there was a jump in numbers, the last of the 23000 series being 25671 and the new models starting at 26000. The new models had the letter "G" on the grille sides as with the A and B, but they did not receive either pressed frames or an enclosed flywheel.

As they were only offered as all-fuel models, the new G models were sold where the gas A, although of about the same power, was not popular. With their extra weight, they were true heavy-duty, three-plow tractors, with some 8 percent more drawbar pull. The PTO shaft had been 1¾ inches (43.75 mm) from the first G, but at 43401 this was changed to the standard 1⅜ inches (34.375 mm). At the same time Powr-Trol was made standard.

In 1951, the GH was introduced with many parts interchangeable with the AH. With the increasing requirement by farmers for more power, the G was selling better than ever, but the imminent arrival of a completely new series meant that neither a standard-tread GR nor a diesel version ever went into production; these would have to await the Numbered Series. The last G was 64530 built on February 19, 1953, and shipped the next day.

Below: The three versions of the styled Model G, clockwise from upper left: GH number 47680; GM 14074; and the last G built, 64530, with shell fenders and Wico XD distributor ignition. The nose of unstyled G number 1006 with the original small radiator is at far right.

A 1953 Model GH. Owner: Maurice Horn. (Photograph © Andrew Morland)

Experimental Model OX and Model H and HN, 1937–1946

With the uprating of the B, the demand for a smaller row-crop model was apparent, so work on an experimental Model OX began in late 1937. The following spring, unstyled models were at work, but by the summer Dreyfuss had styled the new tractor, and in January 1939 production of the Model H began at Waterloo.

The pre-production number H-1000 had been sent to Nebraska for testing in October 1938 and produced 11.67 drawbar and 14.84 belt hp at 1,400 rpm. At the same time, the H-1000 set a world record for spark-ignition tractors, irrespective of type of fuel used, with its fuel economy figures of 11.95 hp hours per gallon under maximum load.

The H tractor's three-speed gearbox gave 5.75 mph (9.2 kph) in third, and a foot throttle override was provided to give a road speed of 7.5 mph (12 kph) at 1,800 rpm. The H Series tractor was equipped with rubber tires, making it the ideal second tractor for mowing, raking, harrowing, and light cultivation. On a small farm, it was quite capable of plowing and other general-purpose jobs.

By popular demand, the HN single-front-wheel option was announced in April 1940. As with the B, the muffler was extended that year. Other options were fenders and a radiator shutter in place of a curtain. For 1939 and 1940, all models featured silk-screened logos; for 1941 and later, the H had black-edged decals of a smaller size than those used on the larger tractors.

Right, top: *Lyle Dingman made this 1/16-scale replica of the Model H fitted with electric starting and lighting.*

Right, center: *Early 1939 Model H, number 1397. Note the radiator curtain, and, unique to the H Series, the air cleaner intake and plug covers. Owner: Edward Daken of Grand Rapids, Minnesota, USA.*

Right, bottom: *The March 1939 brochure for the Model H makes no mention of other wheeled versions, which were announced later.*

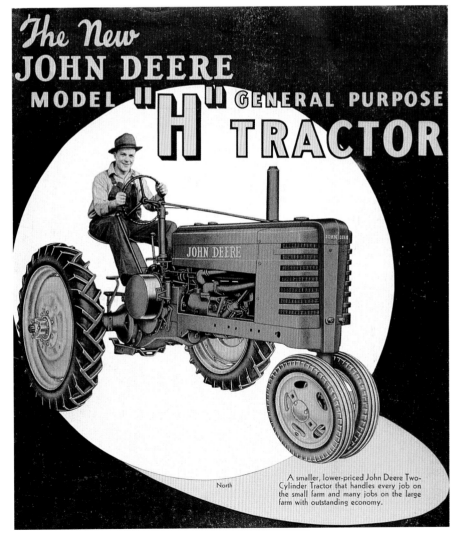

The New JOHN DEERE MODEL "H" GENERAL PURPOSE TRACTOR

North

A smaller, lower-priced John Deere Two-Cylinder Tractor that handles every job on the small farm and many jobs on the large farm with outstanding economy.

Model H. Owner: Kenneth Anderson, USA. (Photograph © Andrew Morland)

Models H, HN, HNH, and HWH, 1941–1946

It was early 1941 before various other options were offered for the H Series. Independent hydraulics for one or two cylinders was the first of these, followed by electric starting and lighting, all at number 27000. At the same serial number, the tappet cover and breather cover were changed, involving alterations to the exhaust pipe and top water pipes.

I once owned an "HW," number 44061, which was an interesting conversion by an enterprising collector. In fact no factory-built HW was produced.

In March 1941, two other models were added to the line: the single-front-wheel HNH and wide-front-axle HWH Hi-Crop models chiefly for the California market. In place of the standard 32-inch (80-cm) rear wheels, these models had 38-inch (95-cm), pressed-steel wheels taken from the B and fitted with a special hub, H991R, to allow it to fit the smaller H axle. Unfortunately, both the new models lasted less than a year due to the war, and production afterwards was not resumed as new models were on the way. This resulted in only 37 HNH and 126 HWH built.

The last H was 61116 built on February 6, 1947.

Model HN. Owner: James Coward of Thorney, Cambridgeshire, England.

Right: *This LI, number 51253, has a mounted mid-mower, electric starting and lighting, and industrial rear wheels and tires.*

Below: *1946 Model L. Owner: Bob Pollock of Denison, Iowa, USA. (Photograph © Randy Leffingwell)*

Models L and LI, 1938–1946

Before the development of the H Series was undertaken by Waterloo, the Wagon Works in Moline produced its small Model L. By 1938, nearly four thousand unstyled L tractors had been built.

In 1938, Dreyfuss styling was applied to this smallest of Deere's two-cylinder models, and these remained in production until June 1946.

The styled L initially had the Hercules motor used in the unstyled version, but in July 1941, a Deere engine was substituted at number 640000. By then, the Wagon Works had become the Moline Tractor Division. The L, when equipped with either the Hercules or Deere gas engine, had 3.25x4.00-inch (81.25x100-mm) cylinders rated at 1,550 rpm, and when tested at Nebraska, gave 7.01 drawbar and 9.27 belt hp. Three forward gears sufficed and the now-difficult-to-find 6.00x22-inch (15x55-cm) rear tires were standard, but 7.50-inch (18.75-cm) tires and longer front spindles created a Hi-Clearance version. The L-1 plow, L-630 vegetable cultivator, L-636 planter, a one-row mid-mounted cultivator, and mid-mounted No. 7 mower were some of the integral equipment available for these flexible little tractors.

In 1941, with the change of engine, the LI industrial version was added to the line and given separate numbers from 50001 to 52019. They were painted industrial yellow with black decals, and were often mated with the No. 7 mower.

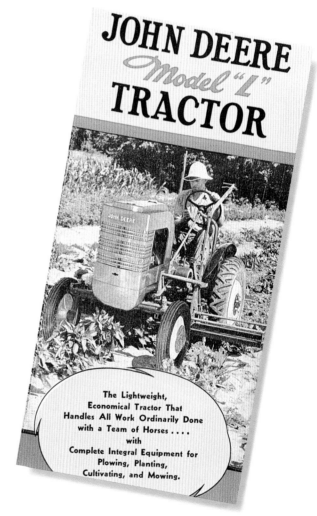

Above: *The February 1939 Model L brochure discussed the many uses of the tractor, which was designed to be Deere's replacement for a team of horses.*

Model L variants, clockwise from lower left: 62 with full fenders; unstyled L with wheel strakes; styled L with single disk; LI and mid-mounted mower; and LA with mounted 2-way plow and belt pulley attachment.

The 1/16-scale replica of the Model L made by the Spec-Cast Company of Dyersville, Iowa, USA.

Model LA, 1940–1946

Prior to the change of engines in the L Series, a model with greater power had been designed, and in 1940, the LA was introduced. Given an increase in engine bore of 0.25 inches to 3.50 inches (6.25 mm to 87.5 mm) and rated speed to 1,850 rpm, the LA's power rose to 13.10 drawbar and 14.34 belt hp as observed at Nebraska. It also enabled the tractor to out pull the H by 100 pounds (45 kg), a rather salutary result for a vertical-engined tractor.

The new model had solid-bar frames in place of the L's tubular frame, and 24-inch (60-cm) cast rear wheels with removable rims; as a result, the fenders did not wrap so far over the wheels. Options included different tire sizes, both front and rear wheel weights, adjustable front axle, two sizes of belt pulley, electric starting and also lighting when the former was fitted. Finally, and perhaps most important, a rear PTO was available, an option that the L Series could not have.

The last models were built in August 1946, ending with number 13475.

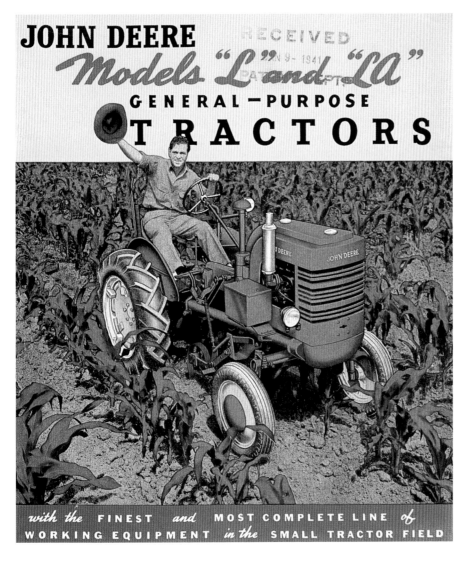

Left, top: *Model LA, number 1001. Owners: Walter and Bruce Keller of Kaukauna, Wisconsin, USA.*

Left, center: *A Model LA replica handmade by Gilson Reicke.*

Left, bottom: *This September 1941 brochure included both the L and LA tractors. Note the LA pictured on the front cover has a silver finish to both the muffler and rear-wheel rims.*

Experimental Model 69 and Model M, 1944–1952

A turning point in the history of Deere tractors came in 1947. A new factory was opened in Dubuque, Iowa, designed specifically to produce Deere's answer to the Ford-Ferguson 9N, the new M Series. The M had been the subject of experiments for a few years. It was designed to replace the small Moline-built models and the smallest of the Waterloo tractors, the H, BR, and BO, neither of the latter having been styled. The M was designed to provide a complete system for smaller farms and a useful support tractor on larger farms.

It was my good fortune to visit Dubuque in fall 1947 soon after the factory's opening. As the only plowman in the party from Moline, it also fell to me to demonstrate an M with integral M2 two-bottom plow, an easy assignment.

Initially called the Model 69, the first prototype was built in 1944 in Moline with a tapered hood that was offset for visibility in row-crop work; a two-cylinder vertical, gas, all-square 4.00x4.00-inch (100x100-mm) engine; and a four-speed gearbox. The crowning glory of the M was the introduction of the hydraulic Touch-O-Matic system, allowing precise control of the rockshaft as in Powr-Trol. The new method of attaching implements was in many ways easier than with the Ferguson system, though it did not have the same depth control. PTO was provided as standard on all models with 550 rpm.

At Nebraska in October 1947, the M produced 18.15 drawbar and 20.45 belt hp at 1,650 rpm, matching almost exactly the BR it replaced.

Production of the first fifty tractors was completed by March 1947, and the last, number 55799, was built in September 1952.

Right, top: *Model M, number 14941.*

Right, center: *Ertl's 1/16-scale version of the Model M.*

Right, bottom: *The Model M was introduced in 1946 after extensive trials through the later war years, and went into full production in 1947. This A-627 brochure is dated September 1946.*

Models MT, MTN, MTW, and MI, 1948–1952

Introduction of the other M variations was planned for late 1947, but postwar material problems and enormous demand for the original model meant that it was the end of 1948 before the MT versions were put into production.

Due to its tricycle form, the MT was provided with Dual Touch-O-Matic with a split rockshaft, so that each side of an integral cultivator could be raised independently. Two options in the MT Series were the single-front-wheel MTN and the wide-front-axle MTW.

The last of the wheeled models to go into production was the MI, which first appeared in November 1949. The last MI, 11032, was built in August 1952.

All the M Series, including the crawlers, carried serial numbers starting with 10001, so that six different models carried the same number, a rather confusing state of affairs.

With five different types of wheeled models to choose from, all types of smaller-operation farmers and local councils and agricultural boards were catered to. The last MT, 40472, was built in September 1952.

Left, top: *A late 1950 brochure covering the full MT Series and matching equipment.*

Left: *The Spec-Cast replica of the Model MT.*

These two tractors illustrate the difference between the single-front MTN (number 26520) and wide-front MTW (40139). Owner: Ross Jackson of Cambridge, Ontario, Canada.

The first MI, number 10001.

Model MC, number 16141, pulling a Ransomes plow.

Experimental Model MX and Model MC, 1946–1952

The missing crawler version of the M Series appeared seven days after the first MT, at the end of 1948. An experimental MX No. 17 had been dispatched to the Lindeman factory in 1946 for evaluation as soon as it was known that the BO-L was to be phased out. The similarity of power between the BO-L and prototype MX meant that it would fill the gap, and the Yakima Works soon began producing the MC.

Tractor base units were shipped to Yakima to have tracking fitted for the West Coast market, and track units were shipped to Iowa for the rest of the United States and export. Similar to the MT, the MC was provided with Dual Touch-O-Matic hydraulics and adjustable track widths as on the BO-L. The new model soon found favor not only with fruit farmers in the hilly Northwest but also with housing and other small contractors.

Like the M and MT, the last MC, MC 20509, was built in September 1952.

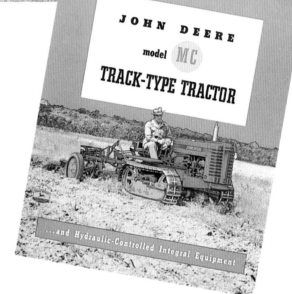

Above: *The June 1950 MC brochure.*

Below: *The Spec-Cast replica of the MC crawler.*

Models AR and AO, 1949–1952

The last of the Waterloo tractors to receive styling were the AR and AO. The style of the R had been fixed early in 1947 with the last batch of eight experimental MX tractors. When the AR and AO were approved for styling, what was more natural than that these smaller models should adopt the same look.

With the new styling, a six-speed gearbox was adopted, with the sixth gear locked out if supplied on optional steel wheels. First gear was a creeper gear of 1.3 mph (2 kph), which was useful when pulling PTO-driven combines or sprayers needing full power. Rear tires remained with 26-inch (65-cm) centers, but 13-, 14-, and even 15-inch (32.5-, 35-, 37.5-cm) tires for rice were offered.

Engines were the same as on the row-crop models. Both models were available as either all-fuel or all-gas; many more of the all-gas were AR models, but the two types were built in fairly equal numbers of AO tractors. The tractors had electric starting with enclosed flywheels and lighting standard, as was live hydraulic Powr-Trol, differential rear-wheel brakes, and an adjustable cushion seat. On the AO, optional citrus fenders, fender sides, and engine shields could be ordered, as could a rear exhaust system in place of the regular side discharge type. The AO also had a shield-protected air intake instead of the vertical AR type.

The first tractors were shipped in June 1949, starting at number 272000, and the last in May 1952, less than three years later, at number 284074. The main features of the styled AO, however, lived on to the end of the two-cylinder era in the orchard 620.

A Model AR brochure.

Above: *The 1951 brochure for the styled AR.*

Right: *This styled Model AO, number 280347, is complete with engine side guards and full citrus fenders. A crossover GP is next to it.*

Experimental Model MX and Model R, 1940–1955

The only Model R imported new to the British Isles, number 4661, was delivered to Dublin, Eire, by the dealers, Jack Olding Ltd. of Hatfield, Herfordshire, England.

Deere experimented with diesel tractors as early as the 1930s. Whether these were adapted D tractors is not known, but various efforts were made to produce a two-cylinder diesel tractor. In 1940, diesel developments progressed, and instructions were given to build the first batch of eight MX experimental tractors.

The first diesel MX resembled the Case LA. Various weaknesses showed up in extensive trials, so a further five were built in 1944, looking much more like the final design. Still not completely satisfied, eight more were built in 1947 and were approved for production with minor improvements. The pre-R prototypes were tested more extensively than most, one even clocking more than four thousand hours in Argentina.

Although it was discussed in 1947 during my first visit to Moline and Waterloo, the R was not shown in a sales meeting until June 1948 in Winnipeg, Canada. Production finally commenced with number 1000, which was shipped to Louis Toavs at Wolf Point, Montana, who is still the owner.

The R featured a two-cylinder diesel started by a two-cylinder, horizontally opposed, gas "pony" engine with electric starting; as Caterpillar found with its diesel engines, the auxiliary gas motor was necessary to pre-warm the main engine in colder climes. Deere's diesel measured 5.75x8.00 inches (143.75x200 mm) and ran at 1,000 rpm, producing 45.8 drawbar and 51.0 belt hp at Nebraska, where it broke the fuel economy record.

The R was the first Deere tractor with a live independent PTO with its own clutch, and it in turn drove the hydraulics. It was also the company's first to be offered with an all-steel cab option. The last R was built in September 1954, number 22293; total production over five and a half years was 21,294.

A brochure for the long-awaited Model R diesel tractor.

Above: *1952 Model R. Owner: Jon Davis. (Photograph © Andrew Morland)*

The Ertl replica of the Model R.

GMW 25 and 35, 1950s

It is said that a copy is the greatest form of flattery. In Sweden, this may have been the reason the Gnosjo Mekanski Werkstad Company of Almult built two models that were similar to Deere's late-style electric-start AW and BW. GMW built about two hundred of each in the 1950s: The GMW 25 was the BW equivalent, the 35 the copy of the AW. The serial numbers of the smaller models started at 25-02, the 35 at TA 500. Several of both of these models are now in the hands of collectors in Sweden and the United States.

Left, top: GMW 25. Owner: the Layher family, Wood River, Nebraska, USA.

Left: A GMW brochure showing the 25 and 35 models.

Below: The Swedish GMW 35 modeled on the late AW. The pressed frame's outline, muffler, front axle, and light position are the obvious differences. This GMW 35 is number TA 553. Owners: Andreas and Rene Felth of Hestra, Sweden.

LANZ *Bulldog*
D I E S E L

Der moderne LANZ-Bulldog-Diesel ist
eine vielseitige Kraftquelle für Feld
und Hof. Sein elastischer Zweitakt-
Motor zeichnet sich aus durch eine
gleichförmige Kraftabgabe, ruhi-
gen Lauf, niedrigen Kraftstoffver-
brauch, h o h e Betriebssicherheit,
geringen Verschleiß und tempera-
mentvollen Anzug. Dazu hat er allen
Komfort für den Fahrer.

Sonderausrüstungen wie hydrau-
lischer Kraftheber, Kriechgang, kupp-
lungs-unabhängige Zapfwelle, Gitter-
räder u. a. befähigen ihn zu allen Ar-
beiten mit Maschinen und Geräten
unter den verschiedensten Verhält-
nissen.

H i n w e i s :
Kriechgang für Lege- und Pflanzma-
schinen, kupplungsunabhängige Zapfwelle und Kriechgang für Arbeit mit
zapfwellengetriebenen Maschinen.

Die Bulldog-Reihe 16 PS, 20 PS, 24 PS,
28 PS bietet jedem Landwirt die Mög-
lichkeit, den für seine Betriebsverhält-
nisse passenden Schlepper auszu-
wählen.

Jetzt mit Differentialsperre

Originally in the blue-and-orange livery, a new series of models was introduced in 1955, including this D-1616.

Lanz Bulldog, 1950–1955

The radiator-cooled Bulldogs—from a small, 13-hp model to the large, 60-hp types—appeared in many versions between 1932 and 1955. Again, war intervened in Lanz tractor production, and allied bombers virtually destroyed the Mannheim factory. Gradually the works came back to life, and postwar Lanz models were developed.

The first new Bulldog design was a 16-hp All-Purpose Model D-5506 introduced in 1950 with a hot-bulb engine hidden beneath sheet metal. With its hydraulic lift linkage, it set the pattern for the introduction of three further models in 1952, the half-diesel 17-hp D-1706, 22-hp D-2206, and 28-hp D-2806. The 150,000th Bulldog, a D-2206, was built on February 9, 1953.

Lanz's 1931 experiment with a twin-front-wheel model was finally put into production in 1953 as the D-2803, the row-crop version of the D-2806. From the HN1 and HR7 Series on, all Bulldogs with the Lanz single-cylinder engine, whether semi- or full-diesels, had the fan drive on the left side. Those with the TWN motor—the D-1106, D-1306, the two smaller Alldogs, and the D-1266 and D-1666 and larger Alldogs with the MWM motor—did not require the external fan drive.

In 1954, the larger Bulldogs were replaced by the introduction of two new tractors, the D-4806 and D-5806 for 1954–1955; these were in turn updated as the 50-hp D-5006 and 60-hp D-6006 of 1955–1960.

All four large models could have nine forward speeds in place of the standard six, giving extra road speed. These were then reclassified as the 16 Series D-4816, D-5816, D-5016, and D-6016.

The 1954 Lanz Bulldog D-2806 had a 28-horsepower, 226-ci (3.7-liter), single-cylinder engine. Owner: Daniel and Yoann Binet of France. (Photograph © Andrew Morland)

A brochure of the two new 1952 models with styling like the 1950 D-5506. Both featured side hot-bulb two-stroke engines.

Above: *16-hp D-5506 with mid-mounted mower. This model was built from 1950 to 1952.*

Left: *The D-2803 was Lanz's second attempt to build a tricycle-type tractor, and this time, in 1953, the model went into production. It had the same engine as the D-2806 and included a 6/2 gearbox.*

Lanz Bulldog, 1955–1960

There were some twenty-four different Lanz models in production in 1955; this number was drastically reduced to nineteen before Deere's acquisition of the firm on November 12, 1956, to seventeen shortly after, and further streamlined to twelve in 1957.

In 1957, two models, the D-3206 and D-3606, were replaced with one new model, the D-4016, which was the largest full diesel model in the final single-cylinder years.

In 1958, the whole line was finished in Deere green and yellow. Also in 1958, the last change to the Bulldog line occurred when the 12-hp D-1206 full diesel replaced the TWN-engined D-1106 and D-1306.

At the end of the Bulldog era, the six smallest models with ratings from 12 to 40 hp were all full diesels with the latest styling. The five largest 50- and 60-hp models were half-diesels and retained the earlier 1952 style.

By 1942, the 100,000th Bulldog had been built; on November 12, 1956, the 200,000th Bulldog arrived. By Deere's 125th anniversary in 1984, the 750,000th tractor came off the Mannheim lines.

Right: *Seen in the Mannheim Works Museum, the last new model announced by Lanz in 1958 was the smallest, the 12-hp D-1206, which replaced the D-1106 and D-1306.*

The 1955 D-2816 and 1957 D-4016 seen side-by-side in the Mannheim Works Museum, Germany. A restored Model GP is in the background.

One of several Lanz tractors exported to Canada, D-2816 number 332919.

Chamberlain 40K, 55KA, 55DA, and 60DA, 1948–1954

Above: *The first Chamberlain tractor to be brought to Great Britain was the two-cylinder, kerosene-burning 40K, number 768. Owner: Aubrey Sanders of Bow, Devon, England.*

Below: *A 55KA. Owner: Greg Baker of Burckup, Western Australia.*

In 1970, Deere would merge with the largest manufacturer of tractors in Australia, Chamberlain Industries Ltd. Bob Chamberlain had conceived the idea in the late 1930s of a tractor built in Australia and designed for the Australian farmer. After World War II, the first two prototypes were built in 1948. The company's two-cylinder, horizontally opposed, kerosene-fuel Model 40K quickly became the leading tractor sold down under. The 40K was the subject of Australian Test No. 1, where it gave 30.8 drawbar and 40 belt hp.

The original 40K was upgraded to the 55KA, which was further developed in 1955 as the diesel 55DA, still using the company's two-cylinder, horizontally opposed layout. Painted an orange reminiscent of Allis-Chalmers, but with a style like the IH W standard models, these were impressive machines. Hydraulics were not required in the Australian market at that time, as the tractors were used simply on the drawbar.

The diesel 60DA was introduced in 1952 equipped with a GM 3.71 engine. It retained the early styling of the Chamberlain-engined models and remained in production until 1954, when it was replaced with the 70DA, or Super 70.

CHAPTER 4

2-3 PLOW ROW-CROP UTILITY AND TRICYCLE MODELS

The Numbered Series Years, 1952–1970

Above: *May 1956 brochure introducing the row-crop utility Model 420 with the new color scheme.*

Left: *A 1957 Model 620 Hi-Crop. Owner: Bob Pollock of Denison, Iowa, USA. (Photograph © Randy Leffingwell)*

The November 1952 40 Series brochure.

The 1952 brochure illustration of the 40C crawler with three-roller tracking. Only twenty-nine of these were made before changing to the four- or five-roller type.

Model 40 Series, 1953–1955

In 1952, Deere decided to reclassify the new models, replacing the long-lived Letter Series with the Numbered Series. First to appear in March 1952 was the Model 60 to replace the Model A, followed by the 50 replacing the B some four months later. Following the 50 and 60 models of 1952 from Waterloo, Dubuque announced the 40 Series replacement for the M in 1953. By increasing engine rpm from 1,650 to 1,850, power was improved by 15 percent.

All the types available with the earlier models were continued: Standard, utility, tricycle, Hi-Crop, and crawlers were built in their various styles. In late 1954, an additional special model, code V, was introduced, which fell between the wide-front 40T and the Hi-Crop, with 26.5 inches (66.25 cm) of clearance against the latter's 32 inches (80 cm). Only 329 40V tractors were built compared with 294 Hi-Crops. Early in 1955, a further model was introduced, the Two-Row Utility, code W; this was destined to become the most popular style when the 420 and 430 Series were introduced. In its short production life of less than nine months, 1,758 were built.

The 40 Series were the first Deere models to have a genuine three-point hitch with exclusive load and depth control, and thus were important to the company's tractor history. Some twenty three-point-mounted and four mid-mounted pieces of equipment were listed in the Matched Working Equipment catalog.

The 40S Standard replaced the M in 1953. Number 70033 is an all-fuel model; only about 3 percent of all 40s were all-fuels. This tractor shows the new-type hydraulic linkage, lights position, and power-adjusted rear wheels.

Model 50N-LP, number 5027135, with the options of alternative fuel and single front wheel. Owner: Richard Winter of Janesville, Minnesota, USA.

This cutaway 1953 Model 60, number 6012885, was used for instructional and advertising purposes by Deere. Owner: the Layher family, Wood River, Nebraska, USA.

Model 50 Series, 1952–1956

Originally intended as an update of the Model B, the 50 became its replacement instead. It was released four months after the 60 and featured most of the same changes as its larger sibling.

The 50 boasted a cast frame, replacing the pressed-steel frame of the late B. It also featured larger-diameter rear axles with adjustment via a single key and a rack and pinion; optional independent PTO; new grille design matching the R, AR, and AO; one-piece hood in place of the previous three-piece; muffler moved to the right side with fitting as on the G, thus improving visibility; and air intake under the hood, drawing its air through the front screen. Other items included a larger fuel tank; increased-capacity Powr-Trol, allowing the use of a 3x8-inch (7.5x20-cm) remote cylinder in place of the old 2.50x8-inch (6.25x20-cm); and a weatherproof speed control lever, with both it and the clutch lever lengthened for easier control. A thermostatically controlled shutter system was introduced, but later withdrawn due to dirt buildup.

Options included fenders, various front and rear wheel weights, a rear exhaust system, either no PTO or the choice of transmission- or engine-driven live PTO, and either 38- or 42-inch (95- or 105-cm) rear tires. During 1954, the fixed front pedestal was abandoned in favor of the split four-stud type; other front wheel options were Roll-O-Matic, single front wheel or wide front axle in adjustable or fixed 38-inch (95-cm) width. Eventually three fuel options were offered: gas, all-fuel, or LP-gas, the latter not until 1955. More than thirty-two thousand 50 Series tractors were produced during the four-year production, the vast majority with gas engines. At Nebraska, both gas and all-fuel engines showed more than a 10 percent increase in power over the same size B due to the improved design.

Model 60 Series, 1952–1956

The 60 Series was the first of the two-cylinder Numbered Series models, the first tractor being shipped in March 1952. These tractors were originally intended to retain their Model A name, but in December 1951, Deere decided to change to the numbered classification. All the various improvements already mentioned for the 50 Series applied to the 60s.

With this model there were of course many extra styles involved in addition to the row-crop. Hi-Crops were available soon after the row-crops; standard and orchard tractors were announced in August 1954. The extra models meant that more than sixty-one thousand of the new series were produced in its four-year production run. The standard models were again divided into two styles when the low-seat AR type was superseded by a high-seat version, an adaptation of the wide-front row-crop models.

The LP-gas option was introduced as a third fuel source in fall 1953, but was never applied to the low-seat standards. In their second year of production, the all-fuel models joined the gas with a double-barrel carburetor, which made for economic fuel usage and sweeter running. The deep-cushion seat and back rest were fully adjustable, the former fore and aft. The six-speed transmission was controlled with a single lever.

Most of the integral equipment for the 50 Series would also fit the 60. An added attachment for all the numbered series row-crop tractors was the new No. 800 three-point hitch introduced in 1953; it allowed fast tool-free hook up of rear-mounted equipment. For the 50, 60, and 70 row-crop tractors there were more than forty matched equipment items listed in the brochure, from plows to corn pickers and cotton harvesters.

New Factory-Engineered

LP-Gas Models "60" and "70"

Above left: *A 1956 Model 60 with non-original chrome muffler. (Photograph © Andrew Morland)*

Above right: *This August 1953 leaflet announced the LP-gas versions of the 60 and 70.*

Left: *The June 1953 brochure for the new Waterloo Series included the 30-hp 50, 40-hp 60, and 50-hp 70.*

Right, top: *In November 1954, the 60S was modified to this high-seat type. Both this 60S, number 6046567, and the 60RC beyond have the chrome-plated "John Deere" on the nose piece as used in all the first Numbered Series. Owner: Stanley Kucera of Nebraska, USA.*

Right, center: *About two-thirds of the 60 Standard tractors were similar to the AR, the model they replaced, both having a low-seat position. The 60 Orchard shown was the same, with orchard parts added.*

Right, bottom: *Ertl's replica of the 60 Orchard tractor is the LP-gas version.*

Below: *The November 1953 60S brochure A-824.*

THE **NEW** JOHN DEERE

MODEL **60** STANDARD

TRACTOR

3-4-PLOW POWER FOR GRAIN AND RICE GROWERS

Model 70 Series, 1953–1956

With increasing farmer demand for more power, the four-to-five-plow 70 Series was introduced in March 1953 to replace the G. Over time, the 70 was destined to hurt 60 Series sales.

Initially available with a 50.35-belt-hp gas or 44.96-belt-hp all-fuel engine, the 51.97-belt-hp LP-gas version was added in August 1953.

Deere's first diesel row-crop, the 51.49-belt-hp diesel debuted in September 1954. With it was also introduced the new V4 gas starting motor in place of the two-cylinder horizontally opposed unit of the R. The new diesel was a great success and broke the economy record of the R. At Nebraska, it recorded the same 45.7 drawbar hp as the R, with 455 pounds (204.75 kg) less pull, but weighing 1,370 pounds (616.5 kg) less.

All four fuel options were available in the three styles: row-crop, standard, and Hi-Crop. Even with the diesel's shorter production span, it almost matched the gas model in numbers built, and the last 70 built was a diesel, 7043757, in July 1956.

Options were as for the 60, and integral equipment was similar but often larger. The standard model could have an adjustable front axle that gave five tread widths from 52 to 68 inches (130 to 170 cm). Other options were factory-engineered power steering, live powershaft, live hydraulic Powr-Trol, the No. 800 three-point hitch, and a speed-hour meter with a black face like the other gauges.

Right, top: *Deere's first diesel row-crop tractor, the 70D was announced in fall 1954.*

Right: *One of Ertl's 70 replicas was the gasoline row-crop, wide-front version.*

Available with John Deere *Power Steering*

It's another John Deere "first" on row-crop tractors. No one can tell you how much this feature alone can mean to you . . . you'll have to experience it for yourself in the field to really appreciate the new freedom from steering effort and driver fatigue that Power Steering offers. Every minute you're at the wheel, tireless hydraulic muscles save you time and effort. John Deere Power Steering will make farming more enjoyable for you and every member of your family who drives a tractor.

Model 70S number 7023417 is a gas version.

The diesel version of the 70S, number 7038786.

A 1956 Model 70. (Photograph © Andrew Morland)

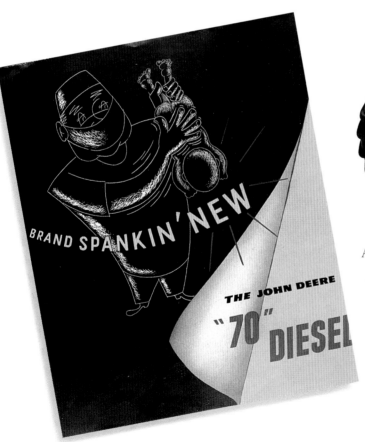

Above: *Ertl's diesel 70 was the twin-front, row-crop type.*

Left: *The original December 1954 brochure announcing the 70 Standard diesel.*

Model 80 Series, 1955–1956

Last but not least of the new Numbered Series was the 80, replacement for the long lived R, which arrived in June 1955.

The 80 answered the continuing need for more power in the late 1950s with an increase from 48 to 65 belt hp, resulting from a bore increase from 5.75 to 6.125 inches (143.75 to 153.125 mm). Engine speed was raised from 1,000 to 1,125 rpm, and the engine design improved overall. The new model was given a six-speed gearbox, optional power steering, increased fuel tank capacity from 22 to 32½ (83.6 to 123.5 liters) gallons, and the new V-4 starting motor introduced on the 70. Again, it beat the 70's recently acquired economy record.

Due to the late announcement of the model, only thirty-five hundred were built before the whole series was updated in 1956.

Model 80. Owner: Dufner of Buxton, North Dakota, USA.

Ertl's replica of the Model 80 does justice to the leader of the line.

The summer 1956 leaflet announcing the 1957 20 Series tractors.

320 Series, 1956–1958

When the first Numbered Series was replaced with the new 20 Series, the basic change for most models was a 20 percent power increase. This meant that the 25.2-belt-hp 40 gas model was replaced by the 29.21-belt-hp 420—more power than the late B Series. The lack of a lower-power tractor resulted in the announcement of the 320 with a 40 engine and M transmission.

Basically two types were offered, a standard, or S, and a utility, or U, with lower overall height that was ideal for orchards or working in low buildings when equipped with rear or orchard exhaust. No Nebraska test was necessary as the 40 figures were accepted. The first year's 320 had a vertical steering wheel; the second year's, from August 1957 on, adopted a slanting version. Just over three thousand of the S and U models were built—60 percent being the standard model—and this has meant that they are both collectible, though not to the same extent as their successors.

The 320V, or Southern Special, with 34-inch (85-cm) rear tires in place of the normal 24-inch (60-cm) and with higher front axles, was sold mostly in Florida and Louisiana. No separate record of the 320V appears in the Dubuque production figures.

A 1956 Model 320S. (Photograph © Andrew Morland)

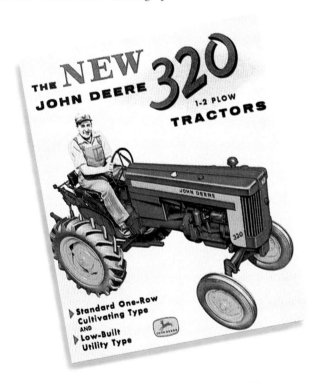

Above: *The July 1956 brochure for the new Model 320.*

Right, top: *Model 320S, number 320916, as imported into Canada.*

Right, bottom: *A Model 320 replica crafted by custom builder Eldon Trumm of Worthington, Iowa, USA.*

1958 320V. Owner: Bob Pollock of Denison, Iowa, USA. (Photograph © Randy Leffingwell)

420 Series, 1955–1958

For once, the Dubuque factory was the first to announce a new model series, launching in November 1955 the 20 Series in the shape of the many versions of the 420. The seven different original styles showed little external difference from the 40 models they were replacing, particularly as the first year's production remained in all green paint with the earlier Numbered Series chrome "John Deere" on the medallion.

From the start of the 20 Series, the tractors were numbered in sequence rather than each style having the same starting number. The first phase lasted nearly a year until June 1956, when the models took the green-and-yellow finish of the Waterloo models announced at that time. At the same time, the choice of a four- or five-speed transmission was added, plus a direction reverser option for all but the Hi-Crop at first, and later for the Special (V)

when this type was changed from gear to clutch operation. The final phase, introduced in August 1957, adopted a slant to the steering wheel for all but the Hi-Crops and LP-gas models, which were introduced at the same time.

Internally, the engine of all phases was increased in bore by 0.25 inches (6.25 mm). Increased compression and an improved carburetor gave the new models nearly 20 percent more power.

Aimed at industrial users, the Special Utility was introduced in 1957, with increased clearance over the Utility. They were only offered with gas engines and ceased production in January 1958 after 255 were built. Finally, only twenty-five of a ninth model were constructed in a joint effort with Holt Equipment of Independence, Oregon, the Model 3-T forklift. One only of this model was LP-gas equipped; the rest were gas.

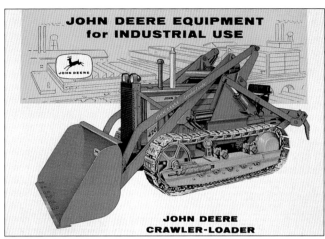

For his 1/16-scale replica, D. Nolt opted for the row-crop utility model and a set of four-gang mounted disks.

The true beginnings of Deere's industrial line is represented by the 420 Crawler-Loader, although it was still painted in agricultural colors. The first full, thirty-two-page brochure, A-1044, was issued in December 1956 by Dubuque, and covered the 320, 420, and 820 Industrial models and their matching equipment. The Utility 420 wheel models and the 420 Crawler-Loader are typical examples.

Above: *An early 420U Utility in the original Dubuque all-green livery.*

Right: *At least five brochures covered the nine agricultural models of the 420 line. This is the first, dated December 1955, and covers the standard and tricycle types in their original, all-green finish.*

520RCW, number 5202630.

520 Series, 1956–1958

The 20 Series from Waterloo were all announced in July 1956. They were fitted with new Hi-Output engines and a new Custom Powr-Trol that was completely independent of the transmission clutch and power shaft, itself independent of the main clutch, and now operated by a foot pedal to leave hands free for other jobs. Operator comfort was a high priority, and a new Float-Ride seat was adjustable to the operator's weight; snap-on armrests added to comfort.

Smallest of the Waterloo 20 Series, the 520 was only available as a row-crop tractor. The engine retained the dimensions of the 50, but its speed was increased from 1,250 to 1,325 rpm, and with higher compression the power was up 25 percent. With only a 12 percent increase in shipping weight, the 520 was a full three-plow unit. On gas, power more than doubled to 38.58 belt hp; even the all-fuel model tested at 26.61 hp. The Model B and its successor had come a long way in twenty-two years from a distillate-burning, 16.01-belt-hp tractor to one with three fuel choices.

New **JOHN DEERE**

520 • 620 • 720

TRACTORS

The brochure for the Waterloo row-crop 20 Series covered the 520, 620, and 720.

620 Series, 1956–1958

The A line's successor, the 620 Series, had features similar to the 520, but was available in many extra styles. Standard, Hi-Crop, orchard, in addition to the various row-crop versions, and three choices of fuel, meant that the 620 was ideal for any farmer wanting full four-bottom plow capability for a medium-sized farm. With aluminum pistons, a stroke shortened from 6.75 to 6.375 inches (168.75 to 159.375 mm), and speed increased from 975 to 1,125 rpm, the new engines had a 20 percent power increase. The need for petcocks was removed, and spark plugs were now in the cylinder head instead of the block. Transmissions and PTO were strengthened to cope with the extra power, and the front-end support was increased in weight to give better balance to the tractor. All this plus the revised color styling made the new models desirable.

Above: *620 LP-O Orchard, number 6212614. Owner: the Cobler family of Ottumwa, Iowa, USA.*

The most important development was the Custom Powr-Trol already introduced on the Model 80: This allowed control of three separate hydraulic circuits. Since the lapse of the Ferguson patents earlier in the 1950s, a new three-point hitch with load and depth sensing was the real answer to the various hitches used previously. The two favorite options were undoubtedly power steering and the new Float-Ride seat. Front end weights also took on a new importance with the new hitch and the consequent weight of the larger mounted implements.

Right, center: *Ertl's limited-edition Expo 2 replica of the 620-O.*

Right, bottom: *Ertl also built a 620HC Hi-Crop replica.*

Ertl's replica of the 720 Row-Crop diesel with wide front. The firm also built a model of the 720D Standard.

The third of the Ertl 720 replicas is a gas Hi-Crop.

720 Series, 1956–1958

The 720 boasted many records in the Deere line: It was the largest row-crop two-cylinder model built by Deere; the largest row-crop tractor tested at Nebraska; it provided more work per gallon of diesel fuel of any wheeled or crawler tractor tested up to that time; and the gas and LP-gas models were also the most powerful row-crops of their fuel type. These were all records of which Deere was proud.

The creeper first gear at 1⅓ mph (2 kph) was a great advantage when operating large PTO-driven machines. Deere's power steering proved superior to the competition due to its greater torque output. Custom Powr-Trol, introduced with the 20 Series, was a 100-percent live system, allowing independent control of both sides of front-mounted tools, separate control of front and rear rigs, selection of working depth, load and depth control with its universal three-point hitch, and increased oil reservoir and lifting capacity. All in all, the many advanced systems incorporated in the 20 Series in general, and the 720 in particular, assured the strengthening of the long green line.

The 720 was only in production for two years before it was replaced with the mechanically similar but restyled 730. With its outstanding performance and flexibility, the 720 was doubtless responsible for the fact that five years later, Deere became—and has since remained—the Number One tractor supplier on the U.S. market.

Above: *720D Standard tractor with power steering and three-point linkage. Owner: Robert Carrico of Madison, Kentucky, USA.*

Right: *New all-steel cabs were available as a factory option in 1957, offered for the 720 and 820 models.*

820 Series, 1956–1958

The introduction of the 80 diesel, leader of the two-cylinder tractor line in 1955, had anticipated the next development, the 20 Series. The first type of 820 introduced the following year was basically the same machine as the 80.

Known as the "Green Dash" models, since the dash was painted green, the most noticeable difference from the 80 was the new green-and-yellow paint scheme and larger wide rear fenders, giving better protection from dust and mud.

The brakes were increased from 9 to 10 inches (22.5 to 25 cm), and the Float-Ride seat proved a popular option. In July 1957 at serial number 8203100, the "Black Dash," or improved Model 820, was introduced with a 75.6-hp engine, replacing the earlier 80/820's 67.64-hp. At Nebraska, the only tractor of any make to beat the fuel efficiency of the improved 820 was Deere's own 720. Other changes were improved starting-engine operation, sealed-beam headlights, and the option of a foot-operated throttle.

A Rice Special was available with deep-lugged rear tires and special brake and rear-axle-bearing covers. These models had a Rice Special decal. An optional steel cab had opening front and side windows, sliding rear curtains, and acoustical lining. Weather brakes and weather brake cabs made of canvas with a steel frame were also available; these could have a heater attachment from the main engine.

The final 820 was number 8207078 in July 1958, but two experimental models took the next two serial numbers, making 8207080 the last. Both the 820 and the smaller 720 had an industrial application mated with Hancock self-loading scrapers—the 720 with a 5-yard (4.5-meter) and the 820 with an 8-yard (7.2-meter).

The brochure for the 820 was worthy of the line's largest model.

Right, center: *An 820 on oversize, 26-inch (65-cm) rears. A 730 Standard diesel is in the background.*

Right, bottom: *A replica of the 820 model with five-bottom plow was made by Step Manufacturing.*

330 and 430 Series, 1959–1960

In February 1958, the decision was made to introduce that year a final 50 Series of two-cylinder tractors. It was not until June—just before the launch in July—that the name was changed to the 30 Series instead. In fact, archival photos exist of the pre-production 350 or 850 line.

The final two-cylinder series was essentially a styling exercise. The last phase of the 20 Series had adopted a slant to the steering wheel and advantage was taken of this to slope the instrument panel on the 30 Series to improve the operator's instrument view. In addition, a restyling of the hood lines, with a rear taper to the lower panel, now all-yellow, gave the tractors a more streamlined, modern appearance. The 330 and 430 U models were offered in industrial yellow with black seats and decals; yellow seats were optional.

The standard (S) and utility (U) models of both the 330 and 430 continued with just the styling changes. Although the records do not show it, there is firm evidence that some 330S tractors were converted at the factory to the higher-clearance V type, as with the 320V.

Optional for the 330 was Deere's special hitch bar for attaching implements without leaving the seat. Also optional were lights, belt pulley, different mufflers and a muffler cover, an air intake pre-cleaner, plus front and rear wheel weights.

Due to the small number of 330s built—844 S and 247 U tractors—the price paid by collectors for these two models far exceeds their cost when new. The popularity of the 30 Series as the last of the two-cylinder models exaggerates their value. The last 330S was 331091, and

Above: *1959 330 Standard. Owner: Bob Pollock of Denison, Iowa, USA. (Photograph © Randy Leffingwell)*

Right: *Most of the original 30 Series brochures had this series lineup on the back cover.*

the final 330U was 331088, both shipped in February 1960.

In addition to standard and utility models, five other versions of the 430 were offered with gas, all-fuel, or LP-gas engines. These included the crawler (C) with four- or the more popular five-roller tracks; the Row-Crop Utility (RCU, or code W); Hi-Crop (H); Special (V); and the Tricycle (T), runner-up in the popularity stakes, which was divided into the usual three variations of twin-front, single wheel, or wide front. All these models had been in the 420 line and were again mechanically the same.

Options for the 430s were more extensive, and in addition to those for the 330, they included a speed-hour meter, electric hour meter, key ignition, cigarette lighter, snap-on side-cushion armrests, and a heavy-duty starter for cold climates.

Surprisingly, the crawler came third in popularity, though with its clutch-brake steering, continuous-running PTO, optional direction reverser, and three-point hitch, its versatility assured its success. Particular options for the crawler were five different track shoes in 10-, 12-, or 14-inch (25-, 30-, or 35-cm) widths, rock guards and

sprocket shields, special wide seat or a deluxe armchair, grille and lights guard, push-pull bumper, and heavy-duty protective equipment and bottom plate. You couldn't be more versatile than that.

Tricycle and Row-Crop Utility models were regularly equipped with Live Dual Touch-O-Matic, and had options peculiar to their types: a 1,000-rpm PTO with the five-speed transmissions, a Float-Ride deluxe seat, and two types of fenders, a standard shell or a heavy-duty style that rolled farther over the tires. Both models had their own individual front-end weights—140 pounds (63 kg) for the T and 155 pounds (69.75 kg) for the RCU.

The first 430 was crawler 140001 shipped July 1958, and the last was tricycle 161096 built on February 29, 1960; how fortunate it was a leap year! The 430s represented a fitting tribute to Dubuque's thirteen years of two-cylinder tractor production.

The last 430S was 160994 and the final 430U was 161017, also shipped in February 1960. Thirty-seven specialized 430-based 3T forklifts were also marketed jointly with Holt Equipment.

Thrifty 2-3 plow Row-Crop Utility and Tricycle models

Left, top: *The 330 Standard model by Eldon Trumm of Worthington, Iowa, USA.*

Left, bottom: *430-HC, number 142103. There were only 212 of this type built. Owner: the Cobler family, Ottumwa, Iowa, USA.*

Above: *The mid-1959 brochure shows the 430RCU model disking.*

1959 Model 430. (Photograph © Andrew Morland)

Above: *Eldon Trumm's replica of the 430C agricultural version with gas engine and four-roller tracks.*

Left: *The industrial brochure for the 430C-I.*

530 Series, 1959–1960

The Waterloo-built 30 Series began with the 530. As with its predecessors—the B, 50, and 520—the 530 came from the factory only as a row-crop model.

Gas, all-fuel, and LP-gas versions were offered, although only 83 of the all-fuel were built. By the late 1950s, the overwhelming choice by U.S. farmers was gas, and 9,264 of the 9,765 530s built were so equipped.

Another major change from the second-phase 20 Series was the inclined steering wheel, which involved re-routing the steering rods under the hood. To protect the operator, new-style flat-top fenders were introduced with a convenient handhold for mounting the tractor; the fenders had twin headlights with dipping arrangement for road use. All these changes were a taste of things to come.

The four front-end styles were the usual twin, wide front, Roll-O-Matic, and single wheel, although the last two could be ordered in extra–heavy duty to use with heavy mid-mounted equipment. In addition to the Quick-Change rear wheel tread from the previous models, alternative Power-Adjusted rear wheels were now available, giving a 6-inch (15-cm) greater tread range.

Options included a rear exhaust system where low clearance was required, a pre-cleaner for dusty conditions, a modern-styled muffler cover, and sway blocks for the three-point hitch.

Today, enthusiastic collectors have created a 530 standard, using parts from larger models to convert row-crop originals and build the model that might have been.

A line of 530 models. The nearest has an unusual single-disk mid-mounted plow.

The Standi company of St. Paul, Minnesota, USA, made this replica of the 530 gas row-crop wide-front.

630 Series, 1959–1960

The four-plow 630 featured the same changes as the three-plow 530 as well as two additional models: the standard, or wheatland, and the Hi-Crop with its 32-inch (80-cm) clearance.

The three models could all be ordered with either gas, all-fuel, or LP-gas. In March 1959, a 1,000-rpm PTO was offered, but not many farmers ordered it. Another option that was better received was a 8⅓-mph (13.3-kph) fifth gear in place of the standard 5¾-mph (9.2-kph), giving a higher field speed for certain operations plus a lower road speed.

The one 620 that was not restyled to the 30 Series was the orchard model, the numbers involved not justifying the amount of alterations that would have been necessary. It continued in production with the 30 Series until 1960.

630LP-RCW. Owner: Chad ver Ploeg of Sully, Iowa, USA.

Above: *One of Ertl's models of the 630 is this single-front LP-gas version. It was also offered with a wide front.*

Left: *The standard 630 and 730 were represented in this early July 1958 brochure.*

730 Series, 1959–1961

More options were offered on the five-plow 730. In some respects, the 730 was a larger version of the 630 Series, with four fuel options and three basic models, the row-crop, standard, and Hi-Crop.

Introduced late in the 720 Series, the diesel-engined version had the added alternative of direct electric starting instead of the V-4 starting engine. This method proved successful, particularly in warmer climes, and most diesel 730s were so equipped.

The last 730 shipped to a U.S. customer was 7328643 in June 1960, but export deliveries continued until 7330358 in March 1961, at which time the tooling was shipped to the new plant in Rosario, Argentina.

Above: *730LP-RCW with integral four-bottom plow. Owners: Paul and Carol Ickes, USA.*

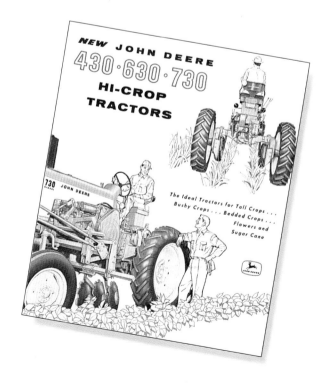

Above: *Ertl's 730 1/16-scale model is a twin-wheel row-crop diesel.*

Right: *The Hi-Crop brochure listed the 430, 630, and 730 models.*

1959 Model 830 Diesel. Owner: Don Wolf of Indiana, USA. (Photograph © Andrew Morland)

830 Series, 1959–1960

The granddaddy of the two-cylinder farming era was the massive 830. With 69.66 drawbar and 75.6 belt hp and weighing almost 4 tons (3,600 kg), it represented the ultimate in two-cylinder development.

There were three works variations of the 830, two standard wheatland models, plus tractors for the rice-growing areas called Rice Specials and bearing extra protective shielding around the brake and rear axle areas. These wheatlands ordered were fairly evenly divided between V-4 motor and electric starting.

The brochure for the largest of Deere's last Waterloo two-cylinder series, the 830.

Above: *An 830, number 8302719, alongside another leader of the line in its day, a Model D, number 178068. Owner: David Lee of Hunstanton, Norfolk, England.*

Left: *Lyle Dingman's detailed model of the 830.*

Don Dufner's 830 Special Mark I seen in June 1993 at his Buxton, North Dakota, farm. The 21,000-pound (9,450-kg) tractor was capable of pulling an eleven-bottom 16-inch (40-cm) plow in third or fourth gear, and a 42-foot (12.6-m) cultivator.

THE NEW JOHN DEERE

435 Diesel TRACTOR

Profits grow, costs shrink when you pile your row-crop and utility work on this money-maker

435, 1959–1960

The 435 was essentially a 430RCU fitted with a two-cycle, two-cylinder General Motors 2-53 diesel engine. It developed 32.91 PTO hp and was the first tractor tested at Nebraska using PTO instead of belt horsepower. The 435 was rated at 1,850 rpm, the same as the 430, but with double the number of power strokes per minute due to its two-cycle design, it had considerably more torque.

The first 435 was built on March 31, 1959, and the last one on the leap year's February 29, 1960.

Above: *The June 1959 brochure for Deere's smallest diesel tractor.*

Right: *A 1960 435. Owner: Don Wolf of Indiana, USA. (Photograph © Andrew Morland)*

440 Industrial Series, 1958–1960

The industrial versions of the 430RCU, 435, and 430C were the 440 wheel and 440C crawler models. Deere's Industrial Division was formed in 1956 and grew from the first MC to the 40C, 420C, and on to these new industrial models.

The 440s were introduced in January 1958. Both had the option of the John Deere gas engine of the agricultural models, or the GM diesel of the 435 on the home market. In Europe, the diesel model had a three-cylinder Perkins engine. They were fitted with a heavier front radiator grille with lights behind it; a non-adjustable heavy front axle, and ⅛-inch-thick (3.125-mm) sheet-steel hood with radiator and fuel-tank caps beneath, all gave the models a clean streamlined look. All the later crawlers had the five-roller track frame, and much-heavier-duty final drives. All models had the slanted dash of the 30 Series.

For 1959, the gas engines were stepped up from 1,850 to 2,000 rpm, giving them about the same horsepower as the diesel models. Sales of the industrial models almost equaled the agricultural, due in no small measure to the ancillary equipment offered for use with them. This included a Model 71 loader, 50 central and 51 offset adjustable backhoe, 63 inside and 602 outside dozer, and perhaps the most popular of all, the 831 crawler loader.

A Pilot-Touch single-stick control option for the crawlers was welcomed initially, and when it worked, it worked well. But when it didn't, it was horrid—and too often it didn't work. What did work well was the two-stick control of both backhoe models, instead of the four-stick of the competition.

Finish was in industrial yellow with black decals and seat cushions. A steel plate with the polished words "John Deere" replaced the hood decals and was later copied on Argentine-built farm tractors.

The 440 models set Deere permanently on the industrial trail, and with their many innovative ideas in design and appearance, they led the way for subsequent developments.

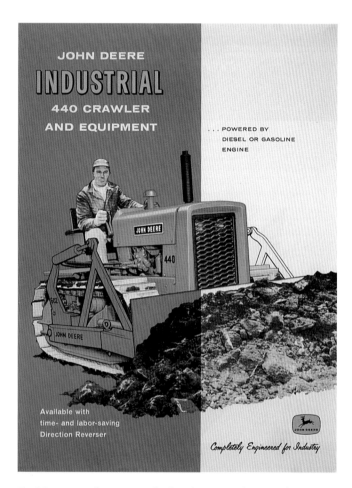

By May 1959, the 440 crawler brochure was showing the GM diesel engine option; this had been added to the wheel unit as well.

An Industrial 440 gas model, number 450616.

The 840 was the first model to have the offset driver position to allow the connection of the Hancock piggyback scraper.

830I and 840 Industrial Series, 1958–1960

The largest of the last two-cylinder models required for specialized industrial use, the 830I, had the front mounting plates associated with all the industrials, plus heavier front and rear axles and drawbar, and truck-style front wheels. Only 127 of these were built.

An adaptation of the 830I, the 840, had an offset operators platform situated midway between front and rear wheels to allow for the goose-neck fitting of the Hancock self-loading scraper. The tractor's independent PTO delivered full engine power to the scraper, completely independent of the transmission clutch and hydraulic system. Regularly equipped with a heavy-duty swinging drawbar, the 840's scraper could be detached in twenty-five minutes, allowing the tractor to be hitched to other pull-type equipment.

Lanz and Lanz-Iberica Models, 1956–1963

When Deere took over the Lanz company in 1956, there were fifteen models in the line. These were soon reduced to eleven. Within a year, two more disappeared, but a new model, the D-4016, was introduced, taking the place of the old D-3206 and D-3606. One further model, the D-1206, was announced in 1958, this time replacing both the TWN-engined D-1106 Bulli and the D-1306 with similar engine. The new model had the gearbox of the D-1106 with six forward and two reverse speeds; the D-1306 had only one reverse gear.

At the end of the German Bulldog era, in 1960, only seven models had survived: the four full-diesel D-1616, D-2016, D-2416, and D-2816 tractors with HE engines and six forward and two reverse speeds; and the three large D-5016, D-6016, and D-6017 models, all with nine forward speeds, but the latter with a 19-mph (30-kph) top speed in place of the standard 12 mph (19 kph).

With the acquisition of Lanz, Deere also now owned an interest in Lanz Iberica of Spain with a factory at Getafe, near Madrid. It started production in 1956.

Models similar to those from Mannheim were built in Getafe, starting with the D-3606 in 1956 and the D-6006 in 1959. Specialized models for orchard and vineyard work meant the model numbers varied thereafter, with a 30-hp D-3012 narrow vineyard model and the D-4016, called the D-4090 in Spain; largest of all was the D-6516. The final Bulldog from Getafe was built in 1963, when the first Spanish multi-cylinder models took over.

Sales leaflet for the nine-speed 28-hp full-diesel D-2816.

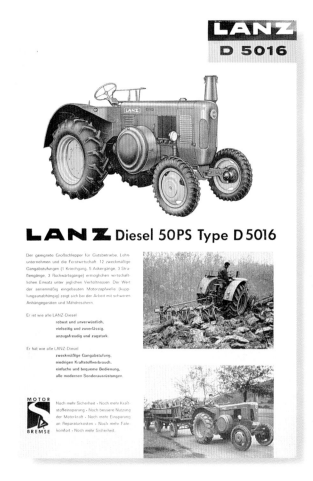

Brochure for the D-5016.

Above: *40-hp D-4016, number 345967. Owner: the Barker family of Westhorpe, England.*

Right: *A D-4016 heads the Lanz line-up at a vintage show in New Zealand. Some of the later green-and-yellow models carried the "John Deere–Lanz" nameplate.*

The sole Chamberlain Super 70 in Ross-on-Wye, Hereford, England. Owner: Den Hitchen, England.

Chamberlain Super 70 and Super 90; Countryman and Champion Series, 1954–1966

On the other side of the world, in Australia, Chamberlain's GM-engined line was first updated in 1954, when the 60DA became the 70DA, or Super 70. This model received a further power boost in 1963, becoming the Super 90. Chamberlain's use of the GM engine ended in 1966.

In the meantime, other developments were taking place. As in the United States, larger tractors were demanded by farmers, and the Countryman Series was the answer. The Mark 1, 2, and 3 Series had a Meadows 4-330 diesel engine imported from the United Kingdom; this was changed to a Perkins 6-354 diesel in 1963.

These new models adopted a new cleaner style, but retained the orange color scheme. Having satisfied the large-tractor requirement, the next model to be introduced was the Champion. The Perkins L4-engined Champion 6G achieved fame as the tractor chosen to follow the Redex Round Australia Car Trial as a rescue and backup vehicle. It was affectionately dubbed "Tail-End Charlie," and was equipped with a canvas-covered cab for the trip.

From here on the company decided to stay with Perkins engines, except for the GM-engined line, until its involvement with Deere.

In 1958, the 6G was replaced by the Champion 9G with a 4-270D engine instead of the L4. Two further models appeared in 1959: the Canelander, a row-crop version of the Champion; and the Crusader, a derated version for farmers not requiring so much power. Both had the 4-270D engine.

Argentine 445 and 730; Mexican variants, 1961–1970

Argentina had always been a large export market for Deere tractors and equipment. The British Agar Cross company had been the importer of Deere equipment since the end of the nineteenth century, so it was no surprise when Deere authorized the construction of a factory in Rosario in 1957.

With the demise of the two-cylinder tractors in the United States, tooling was transferred to Argentina. In 1963, an amalgam of the 430 and 435 was announced as the 445, available in five different styles: tricycle, orchard, vineyard, and two row-crop utilities—a regular economy version with no fenders and smaller tires, and a deluxe model with shell fenders and larger tires.

Finished with an all-green hood, but with yellow panels similar to the black industrial panels of the U.S. 440 Series, and with yellow wheels, they had a smart appearance.

Due to trademark problems preventing the use of the normal leaping-deer decal on the nosepiece, all tractors sold in Argentina had a large "JD" in its place. The 445 continued in production until May 1970.

The tooling for the 730 was shipped in 1961 from Waterloo to the Deere works in Argentina, where production of the diesel 730 in its three standard, row-crop, and Hi-Crop styles continued until 1970, the true end of Deere horizontal two-cylinder production.

The Rosario-built 730s were all electric start without power steering and had the all-green paint job with an industrial-type "John Deere" plate with yellow background and green letters, similar to the 445. The 730's medallion had "JD" above, with "John Deere" underneath, in place of the leaping deer symbol.

In the late 1950s, Industrias John Deere S.A. of Mexico City imported the 620 and 720 from the United States. The firm later assembled U.S.-made components in its Monterrey factory, constructing 435, 630, 730, and 830 tractors with finish identical to the U.S. equivalent.

This rear view shows the operator's viewpoint on the Super 70.

CHAPTER 5

The New Generation of Power, 1959–1975

Above: *The original brochure "Announcing a New Generation of Power," including the 8010.*

Left: *1964 5010 Diesel. (Photograph © Andrew Morland)*

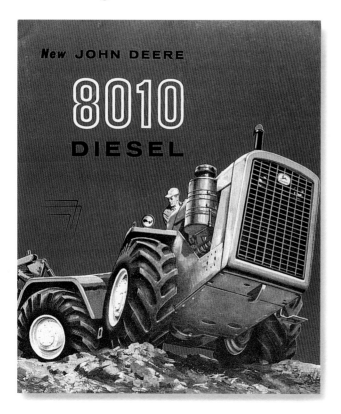

The 8010 brochure.

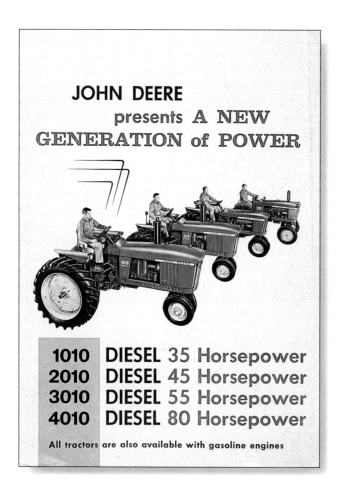

Another brochure announcing the new two-wheel-drive models covered the 35-hp 1010, 45-hp 2010, 55-hp 3010, and 80-hp 4010 tractors announced in Dallas, Texas.

8010, 1959–1964

Although we did not realize it at the time, the first indication of the momentous changes to come was the 1959 announcement at the vast Marshalltown, Iowa, show of the 215-hp articulated 8010 tractor and its eight-bottom integral plow. No one outside of Deere's inner circle knew what this announcement portended, but it signaled the end of the two-cylinder era in the United States and the single-cylinder era in Europe.

The 1959 Marshalltown show was primarily a demonstration of all that was best in the stable two-cylinder tractor world as we Deere enthusiasts knew it, from the 25-hp 330 to the 75-hp 830. The presence of the mighty 8010—"Eighty Ten," as we soon learned to say—did not appear to affect that situation; the 8010 was too specialized, too different. It was also too far ahead of its time, and the fifty tractors produced took a long time to sell; the upgrade to the 8020 was needed to complete those sales. It was more than ten years before the company was prepared to go into production again with its own four-wheel articulated tractor.

1010 Series, 1960–1965

Design of the smaller two of the four New Generation models announced at Dallas, Texas, in August 1960 was the responsibility of the Dubuque factory. Dubuque had an advantage over Waterloo, since the models to be replaced already used vertical engines, albeit two- instead of four-cylinder.

The new 1010 Series that replaced the 430 was supplied with either gas or diesel engine, the all-fuel and LP-gas options of the earlier models having been dropped. The seven styles of the two-cylinder models were similarly reduced, without the Special and Hi-Crop, to five. The first model in production, in June 1960, was the crawler, soon joined by the four-wheel versions: single row-crop (the new name for the previous standard), row-crop utility, tricycle, and utility.

The utility was lower, narrower, shorter, and lighter than the row-crop utility, with the rear wheels increased from 24 to 28 inches (60 to 70 cm). It also had the standard cushion seat, with a deluxe seat optional. When the additional orchard and grove model was announced in 1962, it was based on the utility.

Left: *The twelve-page industrial wheel brochure detailed the many uses to which the tractors could be applied.*

Below: *One of the most popular industrial units in Great Britain and sold originally by all British Deere dealers, the 1010 crawler with front loader and 51 backhoe is the John Deere–Lanz version built in Mannheim.*

All the wheeled 1010 versions had five-speed transmissions; the crawler had a four-speed. The C continued with the four- or five-roller track option, and six shoe options, from 10 to 14 inches (25 to 35 cm) wide, now with four-bolt fixing. Both the 1010 U and C were available as industrial units with gas and diesel engine options.

The matched equipment for the wheeled model included a heavy-duty front loader, two backhoes, and at least six other items, including a 260 flail mower, 245 blade, 250 rake, 255 scarifier-scraper, 265 landscape seeder, C-1 integral disks, and more. For the crawler, there was a front shovel, three dozers, a fork lift and timber loader, 330 sideboom, and a cable plow.

The 1010 Row-Crop Utility brochure illustrates the much lower seating position of this model; the one illustrated is the gas version.

2010 Series, 1960–1965

Although it used the same engine type as the 1010, with the four cylinder liners fixed to a deck, the 2010 otherwise followed Waterloo practice much more closely then the smaller Dubuque model. It was available with LP-gas option in addition to the gas and diesel engines. It had the Synchro-Range eight-speed transmission; three-point hitch, but with top-link sensing, sway blocks, and optional Quik-Coupler; live independent 540- or 1,000-rpm PTO with reversible stub shaft; and an optional belt pulley attachment for fitting to the 1,000-rpm shaft. The row-crop model had an operator's platform similar to the Waterloo models, with deluxe floating posture seat, flat-top fenders with easy-mounting handhold, and twin headlamps.

Apart from its over-the-engine fuel tank, the 2010 followed the larger models lines closely. There was the choice of four front ends: twin wheel, Roll-O-Matic, single front wheel, or wide adjustable axle. The lower Row-Crop Utility model had the choice of straight or swept-back adjustable front axle, and 28- instead of 36-inch (70- instead of 90-cm) rear tires. Optional power-adjusted rear wheels were available. A special low-cost version of this model was offered for operators not requiring the deluxe features.

In 1962, the 2010HC was introduced to take the place of the 430 Hi-Crop, along with a fourth version, the 2010C crawler, in both agricultural and industrial guise. The crawler-loader style of the C sold well in the United Kingdom. The industrial version of the 2010 wheeled model was built heavy enough to include a 330 sideboom with 331 dozer, 340 rotoboom, and 82-I snow plow among its approved attachments in addition to the others approved for the 1010.

A studio portrait of the 2010 Hi-Crop with diesel engine.

The July 1962 brochure illustrated the 2010 Row-Crop without fenders and a 350A rake. Note the headlight position when no fenders were fitted.

A 2010 gas model with three-point hitch crafted by N.B.K.

3010 Standard diesel. Owner: Louis Bartley of Illinois City, Illinois, USA.

The 3010 and 4010 Row-Crop models were covered in this October 1962 brochure.

Ertl's 3010 Row-Crop diesel replica with wide front.

3010 Series, 1960–1963

The four-cylinder version of the New Generation models from Waterloo, the 3010, was offered in four styles with three engine options: row-crop, standard, row-crop utility, and orchard models, and gas, diesel, and LP-gas provided plenty of choice.

The new Waterloo models brought many innovations to the tractor world. The Synchro-Range transmission offered gear changes in both forward and reverse without stopping in each of the four ranges. Closed-center hydraulics gave "power on demand" through three independent outlets: rear rockshaft and up to two remote double-action cylinders. The sensing system was three-in-one: load, depth, and load-and-depth control selected with a convenient lever. The new Quik-Coupler option, first introduced on the 8010, allowed connection to implements without leaving the seat. The lower links were extendable, making for easier connection to mounted implements when the Quik-Coupler was not used. New power steering without mechanical connection between steering wheel and front wheels was standard equipment and was fed by the one single demand-type pump. Oil for the hydraulic system was cooled in its own radiator ahead of the main one. The transmission and differential case formed the reservoir for the special-purpose hydraulic oil.

For the first time on a farm tractor, the Waterloo 10 Series had hydraulic power brakes, which ran in oil so they needed no adjustment. The brakes could be used individually or locked together for transport. The tractors also had a foot throttle to increase engine revs from 2,200 to 2,500 rpm, giving a 20-mph (32-kph) road speed. Apart from the usual options like a weathershield and a steel cab, new ones with this series were cigarette lighter, crankcase heating element, muffler extension, and twin rear wheels.

Again, industrial wheeled models were available from Waterloo with diesel or gas engines, and similar matched equipment. Although experimented with, a 3010 crawler was never put into production.

4010 Series, 1960–1963

The undisputed star of the New Generation tractors was the six-cylinder 4010. Deere experimented in the mid-1950s with V-6 diesel engines and considered V-4 and V-8 engines for other models before problems appeared. The extra engine width for row-crop tractors and the difficulty of dispersing heat with the gas and LP-gas versions soon ruled out these options, and from 1956, all development concentrated on the straight-six option.

Testing of the new OX prototype of the 4010 went on at the newly built Product Engineering Center, located southwest of Waterloo. By 1958, the OX tractors were close to the final production models. The frame was widened from 16⅝ to 20 inches (41.5 to 50 cm), allowing for the new 400 Series engine, which was produced for many years.

Comfort on the operator's platform was a vital ingredient in the success of these tractors. The simple shifting of collars rather than gears, the adjacent brake pedals that could be locked together for road work, and the deluxe seat meant a relaxed and efficient operator. The seat, used on all the series except the 1010, was designed by well-known orthopedic doctor Janet G. Travell. It was built on a rear-inclining plane, so that if you wished to stand you simply released a latch and the seat moved backwards, returning to its preselected position as soon as you sat down. It was adjustable for operator weight and leg length, in addition to its special back support. It was certainly the most comfortable tractor seat up to that time.

With a similar outline to the 3010, the industrial 4010 wheeled model was chiefly used for heavy drawbar, PTO, and three-point-linkage work. In addition, a 740 front shovel, a 648 hydraulic dozer, and the same two backhoes—the center-mounted 50 or five-position 51—were available.

Left, top: *The first 3010 and 4010 brochure covered the standard agricultural models; a second announced the industrial unit.*

Left, center: *An early 4010 Row-Crop diesel tractor easily coped with a four-bottom F610H plow.*

Left, bottom: *Complete with Roll-Gard ROPS and canopy, the Ertl replica of the 4010 Row-Crop was the diesel version with wide front.*

5010 Series, 1962–1965

In 1962, the largest of the New Generation models was announced, the 5010, the first two-wheel tractor of more than 100 hp. Weighing more than 6½ tons (5,850 kg), it was the first tractor fitted with Category 3 linkage and a 1,000-rpm, 1¾-inch (4.375-mm) PTO, a size not seen since the Model G. The PTO was hydraulically actuated with a wet clutch and was independent. Four 6-volt batteries under the platform ensured easy starting, wide fenders with dual lights and an enclosed operating area added to driver comfort, and the deluxe seat and all the controls were similar to the 4010.

The power steering differed from the smaller tractors as two powerful rams steered the front wheels. As with the smaller Waterloo tractors, the hydraulic pump sup-plied power to all outlets: PTO, steering, brakes, linkage, and remote cylinders. New 24.5x32-inch (61.25x80-cm) rear tires were specially developed for the 5010 to give greater traction and the necessary flotation. The transmission was the successful Synchro-Range, with eight forward and three reverse speeds, and a foot throttle increased engine revs from 2,200 to 2,500 rpm, giving a 20 mph (32 kph) road speed. It included clutchless direction reverse in each of the four lower ranges.

Following the example set by the largest of the two-cylinder models, the whole tractor was massive and over-engineered, allowing later developments. The engine was no exception, with its 4.75x5.00-inch (118.75x125-mm) bore and stroke giving 531 ci (8,698 cc). Announced at 117 hp, it proved to have 108.9 drawbar and 121.1 brake hp at Nebraska.

The 127-engine-hp 5010 industrial scraper replaced the 840 scraper. It was capable of 26 mph (41.6 kph) with a full load and had the same off-set driver position as the 840.

The first 5010 was shipped in August 1962; the last was exported in December 1965. The first 5010 in the United Kingdom, 32T 001438, arrived for the December 1962 Smithfield Machinery Show in London; it is still with a collector.

This brochure announced the 5010 in August 1962. At that time, the tractor was rated at 117 hp; this was subse-quently adjusted to 121 hp.

5010, number 32T 5448. Owner: Roy Sapsed of Royston, Hertfordshire, England.

Above: *The 5010 Industrial diesel model.*

Above right: *The new 5010 Scraper brochure of 1963.*

Right: *Ertl's 1/16-scale replica of the 5010.*

The introductory brochure for the 2510 showed the diesel version with wide front transporting a mounted corn planter.

2510 Series, 1965–1968

Surprisingly, a new mid-size 10 Series model, the 2510, was announced in summer 1965 just as the 5010 was about to be replaced by the 20 Series' largest model. The 2510 was the last of the 10 Series and was needed since the 2010 row-crop had been superseded by the "World" Model 2020, which was not available in the usual row-crop form.

The 59-hp 2510 had the 3010 chassis and the new 2020 gas or diesel engine; there was no LP-gas option. At Nebraska, the diesel version achieved 54.96 PTO hp, the gas 53.74 PTO hp. Both engines had a 3.86-inch (96.5-mm) bore, but while the gas model was square, the diesel had a 4.33-inch (108.25-mm) stroke; they were both rated at 2,500 rpm. As with the 3010 and 4010 Series, the Syn-chro-Range transmission was standard, the Power-Shift optional on all models.

The models offered consisted of the usual four front-wheel types of row-crop plus a Hi-Crop. All versions were mirror images of the two larger models, even down to the fenders fitted: flat-top with two headlamps for the row-crops, shell for the Hi-Crop. Most of the Hi-Crops were shipped to Florida or California.

Try its exclusive Independent ground-speed control

Outstanding Features (from brochure):
- 7 h.p. 4-cycle engine
- Ignition key (neutral gear) safety starter
- Fiber glass hood and fenders
- Brakes both rear wheels
- Turns outside a 28-inch-radius circle
- Adjustable rear-wheel tread . . . 27 or 33 inches

Exclusive 3-way ground-speed control . . .
3 speeds forward, one reverse in 7 speed ranges . . . on-the-go speed change controlled by clutch pedal, speed-control lever, and throttle

The first brochure announcing Deere's first lawn and garden tractor, the 110.

Lawn and garden tractors, 1963–

In 1963, a seemingly minor event at Deere turned into a $2.6-billion business by 1998. The introduction of the company's first lawn and garden tractor, the 7-hp 110, initiated what was to become the Commercial and Consumer Equipment Division.

The Kohler K161S engine of the 110 was changed in 1964 to 8 hp, and a hydraulic lift version, the 110H, was added. In 1965, higher-power models, the 112 and 112H with 10-hp Kohler engines, were introduced, together with a smaller 6-hp 60 lawn tractor. Late in 1967, Deere introduced its first hydrostatic tractor, the 14-hp 140, giving customers the choice of five models from 6 to 14 hp. In 1968, a sixth model was added, the 12-hp 120, a second hydrostatic model.

From these small beginnings, the vast choice of garden equipment and specialized golf and turf models make up today's grounds care line.

The first Ertl model of the garden tractor was given the number 10. It is seen here with a trailer.

The garden tractor with which Deere launched its Consumer Products line, now called the Commercial and Consumer Equipment Division, was the 110. Number 2991 was powered by a 8-hp Kohler engine. The first models had the K161S 7-hp version. Owner: Kelsey Equipment Company of Eau Claire, Michigan, USA.

The larger model was the 14-hp 140 hydrostatic tractor introduced in 1967.

John Deere–Lanz 300 and 500, 1960–1965

As soon as Deere acquired Lanz, work started on replacements for the German single-cylinder models. Various LX experimentals were built: The LX-D had a single-cylinder engine; the LX-F featured two cylinders and became the 100.

In January 1960, the first two models to appear from Mannheim were the 30.8-hp (28-PS) 300 and the 39.5-hp (36-PS) 500. They replaced the D-2016, D-2416, and D-2816 Bulldogs.

Both had rubber-mounted four-cylinder 1010 engines from Dubuque, the 28-PS governed at 2,000 rpm, the 36-PS at 2,400 rpm. They had been vigorously tested in Germany, The Netherlands, and Italy as well as being flown to the Waterloo Engineering Center. Styled by Dreyfuss to conform to the New Generation, they had Lanz gearboxes with ten forward and three reverse speeds, and both

Right: The 300/500 announcement leaflet.

Below: A rather special photo taken March 9, 1960, at the Mannheim works after the author's appointment as Deere's first dealer in Great Britain. Seen here is a 3010D-RCW before its announcement in Dallas. Behind it, and announced in January, are a 500 and three tractors with mid-mounted mowers, a 300 and two 500s. Note the famous water tower landmark which survived World War II bombing.

540- and 1,000-rpm rear PTO and a 1,000-rpm mid-PTO. The fenders had a single headlight and handhold for mounting, and a passenger seat and rail on the left fender, a European custom. Combined rear and brake lights and an electric trailer outlet were standard. A unique feature was the sprung front axle with front wheel fenders. The engines had side covers. Both front and rear fixed drawbars were provided, plus three-point linkage with its own drawbar. A tractometer was in the central position on the slanted dash, and a cushioned seat ensured operator comfort.

This French brochure was issued by Compagnie Continentale de Motorculture (CCM), which was later purchased by Deere. Note the leaping deer "John Deere–Lanz" decal.

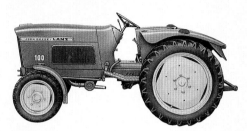

elegant und schnittig in der Linie – stark und zuverlässig in der Leistung

Die überzeugende Leistung, die erstklassige technische Ausstattung und der beispielhafte Fahrkomfort des JOHN DEERE-LANZ Schleppers Typ 100 werden Sie begeistern. Das ist ein Schlepper, auf den Sie sich in jeder Situation verlassen können ... ein Schlepper, der auf lange Sicht modern und wertbeständig bleibt ... Ihr „Schlepper mit Zukunft".

The smallest Mannheim New Generation model, the two-cylinder 100, which like the first of the larger models, had an enclosed engine compartment.

John Deere–Lanz 100 and 700, 1962–1965

Introduced for 1962, a smaller, two-cylinder 19.8-hp (18-PS) 100 joined the line from Mannheim, replacing the D-1206 and D-1616. A larger tractor, the 700 with a 50-hp 2010 engine replaced the Lanz D-5000 Series. Deere's 3010 was exported to Europe to replace the D-6000 Series. Apart from the small tractor's gearbox with six forward and one reverse speed and two-cylinder engine, all four models were similar.

As with the 100, its replacement, the 200, retained the engine side covers. It was increased in horsepower from 18 to 20 hp, and a second reverse gear was fitted.

John Deere–Lanz 200, 310, 510, and 710, 1966–1967

In 1966, the whole Mannheim line was updated, becoming the 10 Series. The 100 was increased to 22 hp (20-PS), given two reverse speeds, and renamed the 200, still retaining the engine side covers.

The three larger models became the 310, 510, and 710. They were equipped with the new Dubuque-designed, Saran-built engines, which would be used in the 20 Series. They had modified styling eliminating the engine side curtains. In Germany the tractors still carried "John Deere–Lanz" nameplates, but for other markets the Lanz name was dropped and these became Deere models. The gearbox and all other details were the same as the original series.

A 310 pulls a three-bottom plow in Europe. Note the new styling adopted for the three larger models.

Right: *French brochure covering the 10 Series; similar brochures were published in English and German.*

Above: *A 37-hp 303 plowing with a French two-furrow, two-way RB plow marketed by CCM.*

Right: *After testing, the prototype CCM tractor was sold in 1967 to a farmer north of Paris. It was found by Christian Hoel, the Saran works service manager, and restored by him to its present state. It has a Dieselair Alsthom three-cylinder air-cooled engine and carries the serial number 276745.*

CCM, 303, and 505, 1961–1966

A French consortium formed of three farm machinery companies—Rouseaux, Remy, and Thiebaud—created the CCM 1 prototype tractor in 1961. A second model was started but abandoned when Deere joined the consortium and built a new factory in Saran, France, which opened in 1962. In 1963, new 37-hp 303 and 44-hp 505 tractors were built there and introduced for the French market.

They were fitted with British Standard-Triumph diesel engines, but were otherwise similar to the Mannheim 300 and 500 models. They did not have engine side covers, nor the large German-type fenders; instead, they were styled like the second 10 Series from Germany with shell fenders. They bore decals with "John Deere" on the hood in place of the "John Deere–Lanz" plate; the model decal was placed on the side of the dash panel. The transmission and seats were the same as the 300. They anticipated the styling to be introduced on the 10 Series from Mannheim in 1965.

Spanish Bulldogs; 505, 515, 717, and 818, 1956–1969

In Getafe, Spain, Deere built Lanz Bulldogs from 1956 until 1963. The first Bulldog built was the 36-hp D-3606. Seven different models were built, all originally in the Lanz blue-and-orange color scheme, which was retained until 1960. Six models from the 28-hp D-3012 to the 60-hp D-6016 were introduced over the first five years, plus the 30-hp narrow vineyard D-3016. Then in 1961, the last two Bulldogs were announced, the 65-hp D-6516 and 40-hp D-4090 standards. Some model numbers differed from Mannheim, but the tractors were similar. In 1961, they adopted Deere's green-and-yellow finish. At the same time, the 1010 crawler was imported as a John Deere–Lanz machine.

The first Deere-designed tractor built in Getafe was the 505, similar to the French 505 but fitted with a Perkins four-cylinder, a 44-hp diesel engine, and, unlike the French machine, with the armchair seat of the 500 Mannheim model. It was announced at the first Deere dealer convention in Spain, held in 1963.

In 1966, Getafe followed Mannheim's lead and announced the 10 Series. In Spain, these were the 515 and 717, plus a vineyard 515V version, and a larger, 60-hp 818. These tractors were fitted with the Dubuque-designed, Saran-built 20 Series engines.

A 1960 Lanz Iberica advertisement showing the original Bulldog, the hopper-cooled Gross-Bulldog HR2, and the new 3850. The brochure promoted the company's long tractor history.

John Deere–Lanz models including this 6516 built in Spain, and a 300 and 500 from Mannheim. The 6516 has two panels removed to show the flywheel and fan drive. Owner: Doug Gantvoort of Clear Lake, South Dakota, USA.

The existing blue-and-orange models changed to Deere green and yellow in 1962. Added to the line was the Mannheim-built 1010 agricultural crawler complete with "John Deere–Lanz" nameplate.

The 1969 20 Series brochure covered the 1020, 1520, and 2020 Standard, and Orchard and Grove models with gas or diesel engines, and the diesel 820 imported from Mannheim.

A typical midwestern farm scene: The 1020 with 37 loader and 78 yard scraper is loading the 33 spreader, which is pulled by a 2020.

1020 U.S. and 820 Series, 1965–1972

The smaller 10 Series tractors were replaced in 1965 by the 20 Series from Dubuque. Designed as a World tractor, the new models came in three styles—the LU (low), RU (regular), and HU(high)—and were row-crop utility wide-axle models. Like the Waterloo 10 Series, they had a "clean-sheet design," taking into account the requirements of the worldwide market, including the United States and Europe.

The smallest of the new models was the three-cylinder, 38-hp 1020 with the new 300 Series engine in both diesel and gas. In 1968, the still-smaller 31-PTO-hp 820 diesel joined the line, built in Mannheim. The two models had as standard many features of the larger Waterloo tractors: front fuel tank, closed-center hydraulics with up to three independent live circuits, eight-speed collar-shift transmission, differential lock, and three-point hitch, with lower-link sensing on the 1020. Later models had a Hi-Lo hydraulic shift option or a direction reverser for shuttle work. Vertical or underslung exhaust was another option; with the latter and with suitable streamlined cladding, a 1020 orchard model was added to the range.

2020 Series, 1965–1972

The four-cylinder, 54-PTO-hp 2020 was simply the big brother of the 1020. It could be purchased as either an orchard or standard, the latter in three styles: LU, RU, HU. As sold in the United States, it had shell fenders with fore and aft lights attached, but otherwise was similar to the 1020. All the 20 Series models under 70 hp had a two-stage clutch; depressing it partway stopped the forward motion, all the way stopped the PTO—a great help with PTO-driven machines. The 2020 orchard model had cowlings to protect the fuel and radiator caps and the operator, and could be supplied with full citrus fenders.

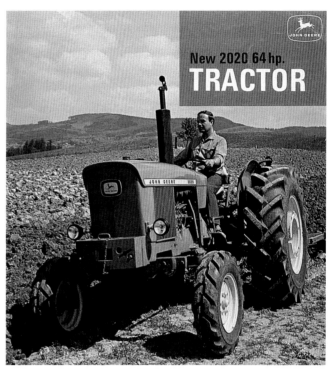

Above: *The new 64-hp 2020 brochure.*

Left: *A 1520 Orchard with industrial-style nameplates.*

3020 Series, 1963–1972

Based on Deere's philosophy of constantly improving product, even if it is already the best available, the 3010 and 4010 were updated in 1963 to become the 3020 and 4020. Increased in power, but most importantly given the Power-Shift transmission option and a hydraulic power differential lock, the performance of these tractors was dramatically improved.

With a 6-PTO-hp increase from 59.44 to 65.28 as tested at Nebraska, the 3020 was available in row-crop (four versions of front-wheel equipment), standard, orchard, and Hi-Crop form. The standard transmission was the successful Synchro-Range with eight forward and three reverse speeds. The new Power-Shift transmission meant that you could move from any of its eight forward or four reverse speeds without use of the clutch. An inching pedal was provided for attachment of implements. It is interesting to note that tractors fitted with the new transmission were the first models with one-lever forward and reverse operation since the All-Wheel-Drive Deere of 1918.

The wide-front 3020 was produced by Ertl for an annual Dyersville, Iowa, Summer Farm Toy Show.

Above: *Brochure for the 3020 and 4020 Standard models.*

Left: *A 1965 3020 Orchard diesel. Owner: Barry Stelford of Champaign, Illinois, USA. (Photograph © Randy Leffingwell)*

Below: *Fully equipped with engine side screens and citrus fenders, this 3020 has a gas engine.*

4020 Series, 1963–1972

Just as the 4010 had been the star of the 10 Series, so the 4020 was the crown jewel of the 20 Series. It proved to be one of the classic tractors of all time, and certainly was the most popular of its decade. It accounted for 48 percent of all Deere 1966 tractor sales in North America.

With all the advantages of the 3020, the six-cylinder, 91-hp 4020 was available in four row-crop styles, standard, and Hi-Crop versions. In addition to gas and diesel, both models could have LP-gas, an option dropped in the late 1960s with its decreasing popularity.

Farmers were becoming more cost and safety conscious, and the introduction in 1966 of the Roll-Gard option for all models meant that the 4020 fit the new requirements exactly. Its 404-ci (6,618-cc) engine—almost as classic as the tractor itself—remained in production until the introduction of the 40 Series in 1978. The standard model now had fenders like the 5010, with two headlights under the front rim. An adjustable front axle was optional; a wide-swinging, heavy-duty drawbar was available if three-point linkage was not fitted. Also for 1967, a fender-mounted Deere radio set a new trend in operator friendliness.

This 4020 Row-Crop model, number 94922, has wide front and Synchro-Range with standard-type fenders and lighting as fitted in Europe. Owner: Tom Parsons of Birdlip, Gloucestershire, England.

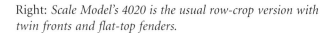

Right: Scale Model's 4020 is the usual row-crop version with twin fronts and flat-top fenders.

Ertl's replica of the 5020 Standard was offered with or without air stack.

5020 Series, 1966–1972

In its first year of production, the new 5020 was available as a standard tractor. In 1967, a row-crop option was added, making it the most powerful row-crop tractor to that time. It had an adjustable front axle, twin-rear 38-inch (95-cm) wheels, and flat-top rear fenders of the row-crop style with two headlamps; external steps allowed front entry to the platform.

Tested at Nebraska, it achieved 141.34 PTO hp and 116.4 drawbar hp at 6 mph (9.6 kph). Capable of eight-row bedding, minimum-tillage planting, or twelve-row cultivating, this was row-crop farming on the grand scale. Options available were Roll-Gard with or without canopy, all-steel Roll-Gard cab, and radio for fender or cab installation, plus the usual front and rear weights.

Above: *A 5020 disking with the new 1968 BWF disk harrows designed to work in rocky ground.*

Left: *Three heavyweights in echelon: 5020 number 12739 leads the team; followed by 5010 number 1439, the tractor that introduced 5010s to Great Britain at the 1962 Royal Smithfield Show in London; and 5010 number 9949. All are pulling Heston big balers in wheat straw. Owner: David Leech, Blankney, Lincolnshire, England.*

Hook up to a new 132 h.p. John Deere 5020 Diesel, the world's most powerful Row-Crop tractor, and...

THINK BIG

The August 1966 brochure introduced the 5020 Row-Crop, often supplied as shown on twin rears.

3020 and 4020 Classics, 1966–1972

The first changes to the 3020 and 4020 occurred at 3020 number 84000 and 4020 number 119000. They included the availability of Power Front-Wheel Drive (PFWD), a first step towards today's popular Mechanical Front-Wheel Drive (MFWD); Roll-Gard Roll-Over Protective Structure (ROPS) option; and a better method of attaching twin rear wheels with wider axles. Patents on the Roll-Gard were later made available to all tractor manufacturers so that all tractor drivers could enjoy this protection.

For 1968, the 3020 and 4020 received refined engines with oval mufflers, a distinguishing feature from the round mufflers of the first models; PTO power was increased from 64 to 70 hp on the 3020 and from 91 to 94 hp on the 4020. During 1969, these Classic 3020 and 4020 models were retested showing the latest diesel 4020 reaching almost 97 PTO hp. The starting serial numbers for the final form of these two models were 123000 and 201000 respectively.

Left, top: *4020 Classic, number 263524. Note the slim oval muffler of the Classic models.*

Left, center: *The 1969 Waterloo tractors brochure covered the 2520 to 5020 Standard, Row-Crop, and 2520 to 4020 Hi-Crop models.*

Left, bottom: *4020 Classic, number 263524, with Powershift transmission and European specs, using standard fenders and lighting.*

Below: *Ertl's Precision Series 4020 depicted the later Classic version.*

2520, 4000, and 4520 Series, 1968–1972

In 1968, Waterloo produced three further new models for the 1969 season. The 2510 jumped from 54.96 to 61.29 PTO hp, justifying a new model number, 2520. It continued to be offered in the four row-crop versions plus a Hi-Crop, all with gas, diesel, or LP-gas engines, and with the PFWD option.

Demand for an economical version of the 4020 with no frills resulted in the 4000. It included a lighter 4010-size rear end, single headlights, exposed batteries, Synchro-Range transmission, and a lighter three-point linkage. By 1971, Power-Shift had become so popular that this option was added. One other version of the 4000 was introduced at the same time, a Low-Profile model with rear underslung exhaust, 3020-RCU front axle and steering column, and 26- or 30-inch (65- or 75-cm) rear tires. Fenders were 4 inches (10 cm) lower, and the lower-profile seat used was from the Dubuque tractors. Only forty-six of this model were built. The last 4000 was number 270280.

The third, and most influential, model announced in 1968 was Deere's first turbocharged tractor, the 4520. With its 1,000-rpm PTO and 122 PTO hp, it was larger in all ways than the 4020. The three-point hitch was for Category 2 and 3. As with its smaller cousins, it also had a 1,000-rpm front PTO. It had a new lubricating system nearly twice the 4020 capacity, a bigger radiator and fan, and an air cleaner, and the alternative Synchro-Range or Power-Shift transmissions were toughened accordingly.

Right: *The dramatic size difference between the 4020 and 4520 is highlighted here. Note the French road-warning lights mounted on both fenders. Owner: Richard Baltzinger, Jebsheim, France.*

Below: *4000 Low-Profile with downswept exhaust and uncovered battery position. Owner: Frank Rochowiak of Southgate, Michigan, USA.*

Ertl's Precision Series replica of the 4000 diesel came complete with ROPS, single fender lights, and open batteries.

820 and 1520 U.S., 1968–1972

The small-tractor line was extended in 1968. Imported from Mannheim, the 31-hp 820 was the smallest Deere tractor on the U.S. market, and from Dubuque the 46-hp 1520 filled the gap between the 1020 and 2020. The 820 was only available with a diesel engine, but the 1520 had the gas option of the other two. Part of the World design was the provision of a mid-point live PTO due to the popularity, particularly in Europe, of mid-mounted mowers; the three Dubuque tractors were so equipped.

This French Canadian brochure covered the 920, 1120, and 2120 models offered in Canada. They were built in Mannheim and fitted with U.S.-style fenders and lights.

The 920 diesel model was built in Mannheim for the U.S. market with shell fenders and U.S. lighting.

820, 920, 1020, 1120, and 2020 European, 1967–1972

In Europe, five models were introduced in late 1967 for the 1968 season: the three-cylinder, 31-hp 820, 36-hp 920, 39-hp 1020, and 45-hp 1120 (Europe's equivalent of the U.S. 1520); and the four-cylinder, 54-hp 2020. Canada imported the 920 and 1120 after a pilot run of the earlier 710 model, but all had shell fenders in place of the European style. Similar to the models introduced in the United States, the Mannheim tractors for Europe had features such as full fenders, left-hand passenger seat, lighting as required locally, and optional four-post ROPS, or various outside suppliers' cabs. Specialized models included both orchard and a narrow vineyard version, such as the 1020-VU.

Above left: European 820 with two-bottom plow with hand-leveling lever. Note the full European-style fenders.

Left: French brochure for the 1020, 1020 Vineyard, and 1120.

tracteur
1020 Vigneron

2120 and 3120, 1968–1972

In 1968, the 79-hp (72-PS) 2120 was added to the Mannheim line, and the next year the 20 Series was completed with the announcement of the six-cylinder 95-hp (86-PS) 3120. The latter engine was a first for both Mannheim and the new engine factory at Saran near Orleans, France. Sales of both models were good, filling a need in Europe between the smaller tractors and the Waterloo models.

The Canadian version of the 2120 featured the shell fenders and U.S. light positions, plus a vertical muffler.

The new 3120 brochure included details and specifications of the 3120, as well as the 4020, 4520, and 5020 as sold on the European market.

4320 and 4620, 1970–1975

In June 1970, Waterloo commenced production of the turbo "Super 4020," the 115-hp 4320, and a replacement for the 4520, the 135-hp 4620, the first farm tractor with an intercooled turbo engine.

The 4320 weighed 645 pounds (290 kg) more than the 4020 and had a new, 20.8x34-inch (52x85-cm) tire made for it, as had the 5010 and 4520. In other respects it was similar to its forebear, except that it was only offered with Synchro-Range transmission. Nebraska tests rated it at 116.5 PTO hp.

The 4620 tested at 135.76 PTO hp and had all the options previously available for the 4020 including both transmissions, but the PTO ran at up to only 1,000 rpm. Three remote hydraulic outlets were offered as well as a Category 2 or 3 Quik-Coupler three-point hitch. Both models were governed at 2,200 rpm, but an override via a foot throttle to 2,500 rpm was available for transport.

The muffler on both models was the same as the one introduced on the 4520 and was now equipped with a raincap. Regular tires on the 4620 were 10.00x16 and 20.8x38 inches (25x40 cm and 52x95 cm), but dual rear tires in five sizes were also offered compared with four sizes on the 4320. Single under-fender headlights were now equipped with dual beams with a foot-operated dimmer switch. A rear combination field-and-road light and two flashing warning lights were also standard.

The 1972 brochure covered the 2520 to 4620 Row-Crop and 2520 to 4020 Hi-Crop models.

Ertl's 4320 1/16-scale model was the wide-front version.

Ertl's 1/32-scale model of the 8020 on twin wheels all around.

8020; WA-14 and WA-17, 1965–1969

The giant 8010 had proved to be ahead of its time, and even when updated and offered as the 8020, it still took several years to sell the initial production. With new models planned, an interim measure was adopted in 1968: Deere marketed the 225-hp WA-14 and 280-hp turbo WA-17 four-wheel-drive articulated tractors made by the Wagner Tractor Company of Portland, Oregon, though they were suitably restyled to match the Deere line.

The WA-14 was powered by a 178-drawbar-hp Cummins N 855, the WA-17 by a 220-drawbar-hp Cummins NT 855, both with a 5.50x6.00-inch (137.5x150-mm) bore and stroke and governed at 2,100 rpm.

An optional cab with either heater or air conditioner was available. Standard equipment included a gearbox with ten forward and two reverse speeds, hydraulic power steering, and high-pressure foot-operated four-wheel air and parking brakes. Either single or dual wheel equipment was available for both models.

An 8020, number 1092.

This photo of the 280-hp WA-17 shows a first attempt to group the exhaust and air intake at the cab corner.

7020 and 7520, 1970–1975

In 1970, the first of two Deere-engineered four-wheel-drive models from Waterloo was announced, the 7020. Fitted with the same turbocharged, intercooled 404-ci (6,618-cc) engine as the 4620, it gave 146 PTO and 127.72 drawbar hp at Nebraska.

The 7020 represented an industry first since it had row-crop availability with high clearance, a narrow hood offering good visibility, three-point hitch with lower-link sensing, and a 1,000-rpm transmission-driven PTO as options. A large selection of tires was available with dual wheels a further option. The steel Roll-Gard cab was standard, as was the Synchro-Range transmission. When it was ordered without the three-point hitch, an extra-strong wide-swing drawbar was fitted. Offset muffler and air intake provided excellent forward vision. The 7020 represented the true forerunner of a continuing choice of four-wheel-drive tractors that are still in the line today.

Early in 1972, the 7020 was joined by the 175-hp 7520. It was fitted with the 531-ci (8,698-cc) engine of the 5020, but now turbocharged and intercooled. All other standard and optional equipment for the 7020 was offered for the 7520.

Ertl's 7520 replica featured the reversed muffler and airstack.

The new 1973 brochure concentrated on the 7520. Note the early decals with the model number on the hood and a leaping deer on the cab side.

1420, 2420, 3420, and 4420 Argentina, 1970–1974

It was not until 1970 that the Argentine market saw the introduction of multi-cylinder Deere tractors when four 20 Series models were introduced, numbered from 1420 to 4420. All were open-station models with engines from Saran, shell fenders, adjustable front and rear axles, and front-mounted European-style headlights.

The three-cylinder 43-hp 1420 was similar to the U.S. 1520 and European 1120. The 2420 had four cylinders giving 66 hp in the 3020 Classic size. Both the 3420 and 4420 had six-cylinder engines of 77 and 102 hp, giving them six- and seven-furrow capability in Argentine conditions. The smallest model followed European styling, while the three larger echoed Waterloo.

The 20 Series models sold in Argentina were the three-cylinder 1420 based on the 1120 Mannheim model; the Waterloo-style four-cylinder 2420 based on the 3020; and the six-cylinder 3420 and 4420 based on the 4020.

The 306 was the smallest of the third style adopted by Chamberlain. A later model 80 Series six-cylinder tractor is in the background.

Chamberlain 306, 354, and Canelander; 236, 239, C456, C670, and C6100, 1966–1975

In 1966, Chamberlain introduced a third design style change that gave its line a chunky look similar to the early 440 industrial models from Dubuque. Largest of the line was the Countryman 354 with a Perkins 6-354 engine. The Champion models had always been Perkins equipped, starting with the L4 and 4-270 four-cylinder engines, but with the new styling the Champion 306 acquired the six-cylinder 6-306 engine. The row-crop Canelander retained its original 4-270 engine until 1968, when it too adopted the 6-306 and became the Canelander AP.

In 1970, Chamberlain's merger with Deere saw the model numbers change again. The Countryman became the six-cylinder 100-hp C6100 and the six-cylinder 70-hp Champion renamed the C670.

A four-cylinder version was revived, the Champion 236, with Perkins 4-270 engine and offered in base B, linkage L, and drawbar DB versions. For the low-power market, a C456 was added in 1972 with a 4-212 Perkins engine. For one year only, in 1975, fifty of the four-cylinder Champions were built with Deere's 4-239 engine as the Champion 239. It was to prove a preview for the next model change.

1020, 2020, 2120, 3020, and 4020 Mexico, 1964–1972; 1020, 1520, 2020, 2120, 3120, 1020V, 1020OU, and 2020OU Spain, 1969–1972

It was 1969 before the 20 Series was introduced from Getafe—three years after Dubuque and two after Mannheim—but as a result the Spanish line included most models from the 1020 to the 3120. In addition, the specialist vineyard 1020VU and two orchard models, the 1020OU and 2020OU, were built. The 1020VU's headlights were incorporated above its grille, and special fenders protected the operator from the closeness of the rear wheels.

In contrast, Mexico changed to the 3020 and 4020 in 1964 with assemblies from Waterloo. The 1020 and 2020 from Mannheim were added in 1966 and the 2120 in 1971—but here the Mexican government insisted on 60 percent local content. Whereas the 1020 was available in its three LU, RU, and HU forms, the 2020 was offered in RU and HU only as well as an additional industrial version.

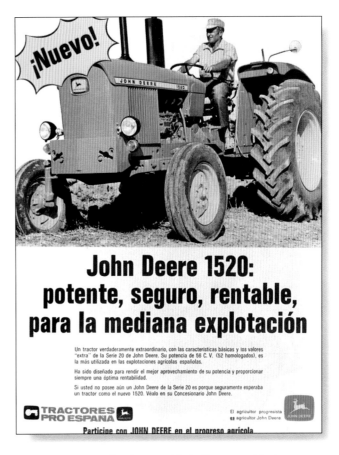

An advertisement for the Spanish-built 1520 with German-style fenders and extra Spanish lighting.

CHAPTER 6

Generation II, 1972–1987

Above: *The September 1973 leaflet announces the full 35- to 70-hp 30 Series line.*

Left: *A silhouette at sunset: A Sound-Gard–bodied 4030 tractor with a four-furrow reversible plow works on into the night.*

6030, 1972–1977

With the introduction of the 141- and 175-hp engines in the 7020 and 7520, Waterloo had the opportunity to equip the existing 5020 with the choice of two engines, the first such occasion in the company's history. The result was the 6030, which still retained the previous model's styling, but became the most powerful tractor of its kind on the market.

All the options offered for the 5020 applied to the 6030; the only difference now was a decision whether to buy the economy of the naturally aspirated 141-hp model, or the turbo and intercooled 175-hp version, which would do the same work but one gear faster.

The 6030, weighing in at almost 8 tons (7,200 kg), represented the ultimate in both standard and row-crop tractors in the 1970s. The next change would be to a completely new style of tractor.

The 6030 brochure shows both the 141- and 175-hp engine options, the first time alternative engines were offered by Deere. This tractor has the smaller engine.

A 6030, number 35776, on twin rears. In addition to a works cab and the larger, 175-hp engine, this 6030 had an extra fuel tank from an aftermarket supplier.

The Ertl 1/16-scale 6030 has the works cab, 175-hp engine, and twin rear wheels.

830, 1530, 2030, and 2630 old style
U.S., 1971–1975

The last series of tractors with the original New Generation styling appeared in the United States starting with the 2030 late in 1971. Built in Dubuque for the first two years, its construction was transferred to Mannheim in 1974, at which point its serial number sequence changed, and the gas model was discontinued.

Three other models were added for the U.S. market in 1974, the 35-hp 830 and 45-hp 1530, both from Mannheim and with three-cylinder Saran engines. The third, the 70-PTO-hp 2630, was built in Dubuque only. It was the most powerful utility tractor of its time.

All of these models except the 830 had closed-center hydraulics, lower-link sensing, an eight-speed collar-shift transmission, and a 540-rpm PTO. Optional on the three larger models was a Hi-Lo transmission giving sixteen forward speeds. The 2630 had more in common with Waterloo tractors: three extra PTO options, live or independent rear 540/1,000-rpm, and 1,000-rpm mid-PTO, telescopic lower links, and a Quik-Coupler hitch, to name a few. All four models had a sloping and non-reflective dash and easy-to-reach hydraulic controls at the operator's right. A two-post Roll-Gard with or without canopy was optional on all four, but while the three smaller had shell fenders, the 2030 and 2630, when fitted with oversized rear tires, had the flat-top type with headlights below as on the 2520.

These four models were built until 1975 when the new-style Waterloo 30 Series look finally replaced the original New Generation style.

The 1971 brochure illustrated the 2030 alongside the smaller models, which were still part of the 20 Series.

Built for less than two years, this 2630 had a low-position front axle, shell fenders, and ROPS with canopy.

Using the 2130 to illustrate some of the variations available, the first studio photo showed the model in standard European trim with large fenders, vertical muffler, and front-mounted headlights, with traffic turning lights under the fenders.

Above: *A 2130 with the OPU safety cab supplied by Secura from its British or Danish factories to Mannheim for fitting there. This tractor also had the new-style Quik-Tatch front weights and hydraulic Power-Front-Wheel Drive (PFWD).*

Right: *A 1974 photo from Spain of the 1030VU Vineyard model with the original-style front weights.*

820, 920, 1020, and 1120 old style European; 1030, 1630, 2030, 2130, and 3130 old style European, 1972–1974

While the New Generation styling continued to be sold in Europe, so too did the smaller models 820 through 1120. At the same time, Mannheim was building the 830 and 1530 for the American market. In 1972, the three new larger models from Mannheim—the 71-hp 2030, 79-hp 2130, and 97-hp 3130—had higher-horsepower engines due to increased bore than the 20 Series they replaced. A larger oil pump was fitted, and an alternator replaced the generator. This change created a conflict between the two 2030 models from Dubuque and Mannheim. To overcome this the Mannheim model, when exported to Canada, became the 1830.

In 1973, another model joined the Mannheim line, the three-cylinder 59-hp 1630, again with the earlier styling in its three standard, orchard, and vineyard versions.

The 2130 and 3130 had two options added in 1974: the U.S. Power-Front-Wheel Drive (PFWD) and the new Operator's Protection Unit (OPU) cab.

Spain too retained the earlier styling when Getafe announced its 30 Series in late 1973. In addition to the standard S models, Spain produced its specialist orchard EF, vineyard VU, and bedded or high-crop M (for multipurpose) types. Thus there were 1030VU and 1630VU narrow models; 1030EF, 1630EF, and 2030EF orchard or *fruiteros*; and 1030M, 1630M, and 2030M high-crop tractors.

The 2130 as supplied to Canada with Roll-Gard and canopy, shell fenders and lights, and new-type front base weight.

4030, 4230, 4430, and 4630, 1973–1975

Just as the tractor world was shaken with the introduction of the New Generation tractors in Dallas in 1960, it was due for yet another surprise late in 1972. Once again Deere had taken a leap ahead of the competition with the announcement of the Generation II models from Waterloo.

For the first time the announcement of the new tractors was made in Europe, at Saarbrücken, Germany, with the whole of the Deere board of directors in attendance. The audience assembled in the vast auditorium viewed on the large screen a film showing a staff member sitting in the new tractor's spacious cab describing its many new features. At the end of his presentation, he opened the cab door, and the audience gasped—the engine had been running all the time and nobody realized it! The Sound-Gard body was born.

Retaining all the best features of the old models, the Generation II models had completely different styling, which again took time to appreciate. The 80-hp 4030, 100-hp 4230, 125-hp 4430, and 150-hp 4630 were offered only with diesel engines in Europe. In the United States, the two smaller were still available for gas, and their diesel engines were naturally aspirated. All four models had six-cylinder engines, a hydraulically controlled Perma-Clutch with virtual lifetime wet-type operation, and the old faithful Synchro-Range eight-speed transmission. On the first three, a new Quad-Range sixteen-speed transmission was optional, and on the larger three, Power Shift was a further option. In the United States, the diesel 4030 had a 329-ci (5,389-cc) engine, while in Europe the 404-ci (6,618-cc) 4020 engine was fitted. Other models available were an open-station low-profile version sold chiefly in Central and South American markets, and a Hi-Crop in both 4230 and 4430 size.

The November 1972 80- to 150-hp 30 Series brochure covered the four new models: the 4030, 4230, 4430, and 4630.

This Ertl 4430 was the two-wheeled version with Sound-Gard body.

A 4630-2WD with the seven-furrow, semi-integral plow.

The October 1976 European brochure covered the 4230, 4430, and 4630.

4430 and 4630, 1973–1975

The 4430 with its turbo engine was destined to be the most popular model of the line. With farmers' increasing power demands, it was the natural successor to the most popular tractor of the time, the 4020.

The 4630 was now both turbo and intercooled. Initially it had been anticipated that the demand for the new cab would represent about 40 percent of the total of 30 Series Row-Crop tractors produced, but actually this estimate was far exceeded, as more than half of the tractors were ordered with it in the first year, and the percentage increased over the cab's lifetime. In addition to the sound factor, the built-in rollover protection added to the Sound-Gard cab's popularity. One alternative, the four-post Roll-Gard, also increased in numbers ordered, so that more than three-quarters of tractors sold had these safety units fitted. The whole cab was rubber mounted, with under-slung pedals, adjustable tilt-telescope steering wheel, and seat belts.

An 8630. Owner: Kenny Kass of Dunkerton, Iowa, USA. (Photograph © Randy Leffingwell)

8430 and 8630, 1975–1978

With the popularity of the new 80- to 150-hp models assured, the demand for an update to the articulated four-wheel-drive tractors resulted in the replacement of the 141-hp 7020 and 175-hp 7520 with the 178-hp 8430 and the 225-hp 8630, complete with Sound-Gard bodies and the new styling. Full row-crop capability, hydraulic Quik-Coupler hitch for the new Category 3-N to allow Category 2 implements to be used, up to three remote-cylinder outlets, and independent 1,000-rpm PTO all gave the new models the flexibility demanded by large farmers. The transmission on both models was the sixteen-speed Quad-Range constant-mesh type first introduced on the two-wheel models. Other features common to both series were Perma-Clutch, power brakes, and closed-center hydraulic system.

Right, top: *The March 1976 A-3 brochure illustrated the flexibility of the 8630 in cultivating row crops.*

Right: *The Ertl replica of the 8630 had twin wheels on both axles.*

1630 Orchard with downswept exhaust.

830, 930, 1030, 1130, and 1630 new style European, 1975–1980

All the Mannheim models acquired the new styling in fall 1975. Last to acquire the styling were the smaller models. In Europe, the 31- to 52-hp 820, 920, 1020, and 1120 three-cylinder models had retained the original styling and model numbers since their introduction in 1967–1968. In 1975, they joined the largest three-cylinder model, the 1630, acquiring both the new styling and the 30 Series model numbers like their U.S. counterparts.

Late in 1976, MFWD with offset driveline was introduced for models 1030 to 2030, the 2130 and 3130 having the U.S. PFWD option.

Europe was still using the full fenders with the new-style 30 Series as seen here on this 1030 with 58 loader.

A 1030 with aftermarket cab and three-bottom integral plow.

1030, 1830/2030, 2130, 3030, 3130 new style, 1975–1980

During 1974, the factory-fitted safety-cab option, the OPU, was announced for the 3130; the 2130 was so equipped the following year. The OPU cab was an interim measure until the new Bruchsal works near Mannheim came on line in 1981 to build the SG2 Sound-Gard cab for all models over 60 hp. The new factory was also Europe's equivalent of Milan in the United States, serving as the parts store for Region Two, comprising the non-American section of the world.

Another option offered for the two larger Mannheim tractors was the U.S. PFWD, which assisted traction in difficult places but had no braking effect on steep hills, a problem in Europe.

A second six-cylinder model was added to the line in 1978 as the 95-hp (86-PS) 3030, making nine basic models.

Right: *A Canadian brochure of the second-style 30 Series tractors covering the 1030 to 3130 models.*

Below: *2130 in standard factory export build, with optional ROPS and rack-and-pinion rear axles.*

As with the original-style 2030, the new-look 2030, when exported to Canada, retained the 1830 name to avoid confusion with the U.S.-built 2030. With the new look, one other model joined the line, a 2030 Multi-Crop, a high-crop version of the open-station standard model. Equipped with a cranked front axle and drop rear axles, it had plenty of clearance for bedded crops. They presented quite a contrast to the low and narrow vineyard models. All these first 30 Series models in Europe had the hood outline sloping to the rear.

Argentine 2730 with Rosario-style flat-top fenders and the usual rack-and-pinion rear axles.

1030, 2330, 2530, 2730, 3330, 3530, 4530, 4730, and 4930 Argentina, 1975–1980

Argentina followed Europe's example and introduced the 30 Series the same year, 1975. Originally six models were offered: the three-cylinder 1030 and 2330; four-cylinder 2530 and 2730; and six-cylinder 3530 and 4530. The five smaller ones were based on Mannheim models, the largest on Waterloo, with an eight-speed Synchro-Range transmission.

In 1977, the largest four-cylinder model, built in Rosario, was added, the 3330, and two further models were imported from Waterloo, the 4730 and 4930, giving Argentine farmers a nine-model choice.

Above: *The initial Argentine 30 Series lineup: the three-cylinder 52-hp 2330; four-cylinder 67-hp 2530 and 78-hp 2730; and six-cylinder 3530 and 4530.*

Right: *A 4030 replica with downswept exhaust hand-crafted by custom builder John Westerveld of Dinxperlo, The Netherlands.*

80 and 80A Sedan Series Australia, 1975–1983

While the rest of the world was gradually changing to the new styling of the Generation II models, Deere, having acquired control of the Chamberlain line in Australia, announced a new series with Deere engines and a distinctly Deere look built at Chamberlain's Welshpool factory. The new 80 Sedan Series of 1975—"sedan" being Australian for a fitted cab—were sharp tractors with a new yellow paint finish, an optional safety cab that looked similar to the European OPU, and a six-post protective frame. The new models gave the company a 21 percent share of the Australian market, making it the largest tractor supplier on the continent.

The four standard models in the line were a four-cylinder 239-ci (3,915-cc) 3380, and three six-cylinder models: the 329-ci (5,389-cc) 4080, the 359 ci (5,880-cc) 4280, and turbo 4480. All were powered by Deere engines from Saran with ratings of 68, 85, 98, and 119 PTO hp respectively.

The 4080 could be purchased as a cane or row-crop model, with adjustable front and rear axles, and a six-post ROPS frame in place of the cab. A hydraulic live PTO was standard on all models, while Category 2 three-point linkage was standard on the 3380 and 4080 cane model, and optional on the standard 4080 and 4280.

Chamberlain 4480 replica from John Westerveld of Dinxperlo, The Netherlands.

Smallest of the six-cylinder models, the 4080 mustered 85 PTO hp.

The middle of the Chamberlain six-cylinder models, the 4280, was the Australian equivalent of the U.S. 4430 Series.

The second series brochures for the Chamberlain 80 Series had the largest model, the 119-PTO-hp 4480, on the cover.

4235, 4435, 2535, and 2735 Mexico, 1973–1983; 1035, 1635, 2035, 2135, and 3135 Spain, 1977–1980

In 1973, the first 35 Series tractor was announced in Mexico, the 4435. It was joined the next year by the 4235, both with the new styling. In Spain and other Spanish-speaking markets like Mexico, the new styling was delayed on the smaller models until 1977, when it also appeared as the 35 Series. Similar models to the original-style 30 Series were available in Spain except the 1035 in high-crop M form; in Mexico the four-cylinder 2535 and 2735, built in Saltillo, joined the line in 1975. The 35 Series had the same engine power as the 30 Series it replaced, and stayed in production until 1980 in Spain and 1983 in Mexico. The Mexican models adopted the flat-top fenders from the United States, both with and without lights.

The 4435 was assembled from units imported from Waterloo. John Westerveld's model was handmade.

Mexican 2735 with various homemade accessories, including the canopy.

2040, 2240, 2440, and 2640
old style U.S., 1975–1979

The new styling that was introduced by Waterloo for the 30 Series two- and four-wheel-drive models was adopted for the under-75-hp models in summer 1975. The three-cylinder 2040 and 2240 replaced the 830 and 1530, providing an extra 5 hp each, and were still supplied from Mannheim.

The four-cylinder 2440 and 2640 replaced the 2030 and 2630 with no increase in power and were still built in Dubuque. Apart from their engines, all four new models came one step nearer to their larger row-crop cousins with such standard features as power steering, hydraulic brakes, lower-link sensing, differential lock, fully adjustable swinging drawbar, and live PTO.

The largest four-cylinder 40 Series model, the 2640, was still built in Dubuque.

An early 40 Series brochure covering Deere's lineup, from the 40-hp 2040 to the 70-hp 2640.

A 2040 40-hp Utility with offset MFWD.

Ertl's replica of an open-station 2640 with front loader.

2040, 2240, 2440, 2640, and 2840, 1975–1979

Orchard and vineyard versions of the 2240 were built in both Mannheim and Getafe, and were both low and narrow respectively for their specialized operations.

The four 2040, 2240, 2440, and 2640 models were all available as orchard models, with low silhouettes, downswept exhausts, shell fenders, straight or swept-back front axles for shorter turning, and small-diameter rear wheels.

During 1976, the six-cylinder 80-hp 2840 was added to the line. It had a 329-ci (5,389-cc) diesel engine and a twelve-speed Hi-Lo transmission. It retained the closed-center hydraulics, Category 2 lower-link-sensing three-point hitch, two remote cylinder outlets, and hydraulically engaged independent 540/1,000-rpm PTO. In line with current practice, it had a differential lock, U.S.-style rack-and-pinion rear axles, and flat-top fenders. Built in Mannheim, it was a true "small big" tractor with many of the other 40 Series parts interchangeable.

Left, top: *This brochure covers the orchard and grove models with the later style.*

Left, center: *Disking between the trees, this 2640-O orchard model is one of the first 40 series with rear-sloping hood.*

Left, bottom: *This 80-hp 2840 with 4-bottom semi-mounted plow is also the first 40 style.*

850 and 950, 1977–1989

In the late 1970s, tractors with less than 40 hp could be built more economically in Japan than in the United States, so Deere, like most of the major tractor manufacturers, decided to follow this course. For 1978, the 850 and 950 "small big" tractors were announced, the result of prolonged negotiations with the Japanese company Yanmar. They were the first of a line of seven models eventually built in Japan with three-cylinder Deere engines.

These first two had 22 and 27 PTO hp with eight-speed transmissions with two-lever control and a differential lock that could be engaged on the go. Their 540-rpm PTO had an overrunning clutch, while the linkage was Category 1. A variety of implements were developed to work with this new line for agricultural and truck farmers, professional grounds keepers, and nurseries.

The first brochure issued for the 22-hp 850 and 27-hp 950 built by Yanmar in Japan. Note the Quik-Tatch front weights that simply lift from their frame.

A later brochure for the 850 and 950.

The 950 was modeled by Ertl in 1/16 scale complete with rollbar.

4040, 4240, 4440, 4640, and 4840 U.S.; 8440 and 8640, 1978–1982

Late in 1977, for the 1978 season, Deere announced a new line of row-crop tractors called the "Iron Horses" because they had more power and more iron than the series they replaced. They were the 40 Series from Waterloo, and there were now five models, the 180-hp 4840 having been added to the top of the line. Greater drawbar pull and increased lift capacity answered the farmer's continued request for ever more power.

Originally thought to have ended with the 30 Series, it is now known that a twin tricycle-front with four-bolt pedestal fixing could be ordered on at least the 4040. Jim Birk of Hutchinson, Minnesota, received one, number 11759, on October 1, 1981. It was later converted to the normal four-wheel, wide-front form.

The new models had from 14 to 29 percent more lifting ability, and if the optional external lift cylinders were supplied for the three smaller models, this was increased to more than 50 percent. The operator was not forgotten: New seats with HydraCushioned suspension, which reduced bumps and jolts hydraulically, were available, and even better sound-deadening materials were added to reduce the cab noise levels. The 4640 tied the all-time record low in official sound tests at 77.5 decibels.

When first tested, the 4040 was rated at 90 hp, the 4240 at 110 hp, the 4440 at 130 hp, the 4640 at 156 hp, and the 4840 at 180 hp at the PTO.

The four-wheel-drive articulated 8440 and 8640 were updated for 1979, with slightly increased power with many small internal detail changes but little external items to illustrate this.

Left: *Plowing in Europe with a four-furrow, two-way plow, this 4240 has hydraulic PFWD and Sound-Gard body.*

Below: *The initial brochure covering the new 40 Series promoted them as the "Iron Horses."*

Above: *The comprehensive A-1 brochure from September 1981.*

The November 1978 brochure listed the 1979 215-hp 8440 and 275-hp 8640.

A 4440 plowing alfalfa. Owner: the Kroneman family.

John Westerveld's 1/32-scale handmade model of a 4240 Hi-Crop.

Ertl's 8640 was on twin wheels befitting the largest of the 40 Series models.

Ertl's 4440 model was complete with Sound-Gard body.

Hard at work ripping up stubble, this 8640 was on twin wheels all around.

The 4040 shown was delivered to the Birks in 1981 with this 8640, which is waiting for fitting of its twin wheels.

840, 940, 1040, 1140, and 1640 new-style up-slope Europe, 1979–1982; 2940 new-style up-slope U.S. 1980–1982; A Centre MFWD 1983–

The rest of the U.S. tractor line from Mannheim and Dubuque conformed to the styling adopted for Waterloo models in 1979 because the new Bruchsal factory was soon due to produce the SG2 Sound-Gard body, which required a hood that rose toward the rear in place of the existing hood that sloped down to the rear. All versions, whether with cab or open station, vineyard, orchard, or high-crop, adopted this hood style. With the new styling, the models were introduced in the United States, as New Profiles of Performance; in Europe they were called the Schedule Masters since they could deliver more work in a given time.

The largest U.S. model became the 2940 with the new styling and a larger engine of 359-ci (5,880-cc) capacity, replacing the 2840. The Mannheim-built 2040, 2240, and 2940 had Top-Shaft-Synchronized (TSS) transmissions as an option on the two smaller models and standard on the 2940. From 1977, an MFWD option was available with off-center driveshaft with a front tie rod, from an outside supplier. In 1983, a center-drive-line version replaced the earlier design, and incorporated a 12-degree caster/action MFWD. The 2940 was the first of these five models to be offered with the SG2 option, and its standard TSS transmission gave sixteen forward and eight reverse speeds. Tested at Nebraska, it gave 81.17 PTO hp.

Most Spanish tractors were open station and carried the European numbering system with added letters to define their purpose. The 40 Series lettering used F for orchard, or *fruiteros*; V for vineyard; M for high-crop, or multi-purpose; and S-2 and S-4 for standard two- and four-wheel drive.

This 2940 MFWD has both the new styling and center drive to the front wheels.

GENETIC ENGINEERING

Here's how John Deere uses 'genetic engineering' to make these 40- to 80-hp tractors more productive

Deere's commitment to "genetic engineering" was explained as applied to the 40 Series.

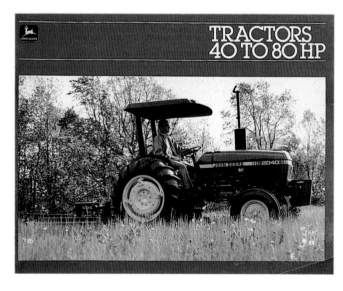

Above: *The 2040 Low-Profile replicated by John Westerveld.*

Left: *The main brochure covered the original line from the 2040 to 2940.*

A 2140 in charge of a Ransomes beet harvester; a 3350 attends with a TF dump trailer. Owner: James Coward of Thorney, near Peterborough, England.

40 Series U.S., Europe, and Canada, 1979–1986

When the new-style 40 Series arrived in late 1979 as 1980 models in Europe, both the European and U.S. tractors had 40 Series numbers but different model numbering. The U.S. models were 2040, 2240, 2440, 2640, and 2940; the equivalent European tractors were 1040, 1140, 2040, 2140, and 3140. Canadian models followed Europe, except the 2040 became the 1840 to save confusion with the three-cylinder U.S. model.

The European market also demanded extra models. The 840 and 940 were small, three-cylinder tractors, while the four-cylinder 1640 and six-cylinder 3040 were derated versions of the 2040 and 3140. All models from the 1640 up the line had the SG2 cab option and a new central-driveline MFWD. All Mannheim and Getafe models had the muffler under the hood, allowing a slim straight pipe above for improved forward visibility.

In 1983, economic depression hit European agriculture, so Mannheim announced a low-priced series of three models, the revised LP-gas version of the 1640, 2040, and 2140.

A 1040V spraying a Spanish vineyard.

The 1984, 123-hp (112-PS) 3640 was Deere's first tractor with MFWD standard. The 3640 also boasted optional front linkage and a 1,000-rpm front PTO, giving the Mannheim line an extra top-of-the-range six-cylinder model with exclusive features. A 16/8 Power Synchron transmission with Hi-Lo shifting was standard. The versatility of this new model set new standards.

A six-cylinder 3040 on haulage duty. Owner: the Whitting family, near Gloucester, England.

Brochure announcing the 112-hp 3640 with MFWD standard and optional front PTO and hitch.

The Canadian brochure covering the 1040 to 3140, plus the 1140 Orchard/Vineyard.

The 3140 model had the Sound-Gard 2 (SG2) cab and four-wheel drive.

2040S, 4040S, 4240S, and 4350; X-E Series, 1982–1986

When the 50 Series was announced in the United States in 1981, the 2040 was uprated in Europe from 70 to 75 hp and reclassified as the 2040S. Similarly, the Waterloo 4040 and 4240, which were assembled in Mannheim and "Europeanized," were also uprated 5 hp, and became the 4040S and 4240S.

The 4240S was replaced for one year in 1985 by the 4350. It featured an 8-hp increase, the hydraulic system pressure raised from 2,250 to 2,496 psi, and three-point linkage now Category 3N as well as Category 2.

For 1984, inexpensive X-E Series versions of the 1640, 2040, 2040S, and 2140 were introduced with the same options as the standard models. They were offered to aid farmers in coping with the difficult economic times.

Tractores 2040 Linea Super

The Getafe-built models in the S Series, such as this 2040-MFWD with SG2 cab, were referred to as the "Supers."

This 1640-MFWD X-E model had a low-profile SG2 cab for working in low buildings and a Swedish-made Quicke front loader.

The Mannheim-assembled 4240S was the largest model of the S Series.

Above left: *The 1982 2040S brochure.*

Above right: *Showing the front mudguards available in Europe for both two- and four-wheel drive tractors, the 1640 X-E leaflet was dated October 1985.*

Left: *John Westerveld's 1/32-scale model of the 4040S-MFWD with SG2 cab is complete with radio aerial.*

1140, 2040, 2140, 3140, 3340, 3540, 4040, and 4050 Argentina, 1981–1987

In Argentina, the 40 Series was introduced in 1981, following the European styling of hood and muffler, but the models retained their own flat-top fenders with a single headlight below on the larger models, shell-type on the smaller.

The 1140 and 2040 were imported from Mannheim. Initially, the 2140 and 3140 were also imported, but from 1983, they were built in Rosario. The 3540 was a six-cylinder turbo version of the 3140 introduced in 1986. The large 4040 was imported from Waterloo. From 1984 to 1987, the 4040 was replaced by the 4050.

The 3140 Super built in Getafe with its SG2 cab makes an interesting contrast with the open-station 2140 and 3540 built in Rosario, Argentina.

The 3540 was equipped with center-drive MFWD as standard. The 3340 had the option of two- or four-wheel drive.

1641, 2541, 2941, 3141, and 3641
South Africa, 1982–1986

In 1982, the Nigel works in South Africa produced its first "homemade" tractors, the 41 Series, the last of Deere's 40 Series to be introduced. The South African government ordained that tractors built in the country must contain a certain percentage of local parts; thus, the locally produced Atlantis Diesel Engine Company (ADE) engines, a Perkins subsidiary, were used in the new models.

The 41 Series was similar in other respects to the Mannheim 40 Series, and consisted of five sizes and eleven models: the four-cylinder 1641 and 1641F orchard naturally aspirated models; the altitude-compensated 2141; the turbo 2541 and 2941; and the altitude-compensated, six-cylinder 3141. All except the 1641F were available with two-wheel or MFWD. The ADE engines used 175 different parts compared to the Deere-engined models, but it enabled the company to take fourth place in the market in its first year. Normal specification was open station with shell fenders and electric lights fore and aft.

Left, top: *The leader of the 41 Series, the 3641-MFWD, complete with two-post ROPS and canopy.*

Left, bottom: *The 1984 41 Series brochure illustrated all six basic models in different guises on its cover.*

1050, 650, and 750, 1980–

In late 1979, a third member of the Yanmar-built 50 Series appeared, the 1050. Similar in appearance to the first two models, its three-cylinder engine was turbocharged, giving 33.41 PTO hp at Nebraska. With its extra power, it was fitted with a load-sensing three-point hitch.

In 1980, the 17-hp 650 and 20-hp 750 joined the Compact Utility line, the former with a two-cylinder diesel engine. MFWD, front PTO, and power steering were optional on all of these tractors.

Above: *The four smallest models of the 50 Series Yanmar line: the 14.5-PTO-hp 650, 18-hp 750, 22-hp 850, and 27-hp 950.*

Left: *950-MFWD complete with ROPS and canopy.*

A 750 mounted with a 272 grooming mower on the front of a compact utility tractor brochure.

CHAPTER 7

The Modern Years, 1982–1991

Above: *"New Firepower": December 1988 brochure for the full 55 Series line from the 4055 to the 4955.*

Left: *The 1984 8850. Owner: Ruth Schaefer of Grabill, Indiana, USA. (Photograph © Andrew Morland)*

Above: *A 50 Series brochure introduces the series with a belt buckle as its central motive, indicating a belt-tightening operation with the new models.*

Below: *A long entourage of 9000 Series drills means a lot of drilling in a day with an 8850 in charge.*

8450, 8650, and 8850, 1982–1988

The year 1982 saw a number of interesting developments in the makeup of the Deere tractor line. New four-wheel-drive articulated tractors were announced; the previous two-model line was extended to three as the 8450 and 8650 superseded the 40 Series with an extra 7 and 10 PTO hp respectively; and the all-new V-8–engined 8850 was rated at 303.99 PTO hp when tested. The 8850 was the most powerful tractor the company had produced up to that time. It had a Category 4 or 4N hitch, and a temperature-sensing viscous fan drive that reduced fan speed when temperatures dropped. It had a distinctive deep front grille. All three models had their exhaust and air intakes moved to the cab corner for improved forward vision.

Below: *Ertl chose the 8650 on twins as its 50 Series four-wheel-drive model.*

1250, 1450, 1650, and 900HC, 1982–1986

The 40-hp 1250 was added to the five tractors in the Yanmar line. The 1250 was still a three-cylinder, naturally aspirated tractor, and like the smaller models could be two- or four-wheel drive. In 1984, the four-cylinder 1450 and 1650 joined this lengthening line, the latter with turbo. When they were tested at Nebraska, the three models broke a total of nine economy and lugging records. The largest model was the most fuel-efficient tractor ever tested, regardless of horsepower, and it set four other records in the 55-to-65-hp class. The 1450 collected three records in the 45-to-55-hp class, and the 1250 collected a lugging record in its class. The three tractors were sold as 40-, 50-, and 60-PTO-hp machines, although they exceeded these figures on test.

The specialist 900HC came from the Yanmar connection in 1986 with 25 gross engine horsepower. It had 23 inches (57.5 cm) of clearance under the front axle, 27 inches (67.5 cm) under the rear, and with its offset seating position, it had excellent visibility for the operator. It was aimed at farmers with truck gardens, nurseries, and strawberry or tobacco fields. It was fitted as standard with an eight-speed transmission, continuous live 540-rpm PTO, differential lock, Category 1 linkage, and adjustable front axle.

Above, top: *The 1450 and 1650 had a first front weight similar to the larger series rather than the weight tray of this series's six smaller models.*

Above, bottom: *The four larger Yanmar-built 37- to 60-hp models, illustrating the two- and four-wheel-drive options.*

4050, 4250, 4450, 4650, and 4850, 1982–1986

Below, top: *The French brochure for the Waterloo-built 50 Series covered the full 4050 to 4850 range.*

Below, bottom: *U.S. 4450-MFWD.*

In late 1982, Deere announced its largest new model lineup in the firm's history in the United States. This was the 50 Series, with five models each from Mannheim and Waterloo. The larger, Waterloo-built models and their PTO power ratings were the 100-hp 4050, 120-hp 4250, 140-hp 4450, 165-hp 4650, and 190-hp 4850.

All ten models had a new center-line mechanical-front-wheel drive (MFWD) as an option, with a patented Caster-Action, allowing the front wheels to caster 13 degrees and tilt, allowing tighter turns.

A new fifteen-speed Power Shift transmission was available for the Waterloo tractors; four speeds under 3 mph (4.8 kph) for PTO work, seven for general field work, and four for transport speeds. The Power Shift was standard on the 4850; Quad-Range was standard on the other four. The 4250 was also offered as a Hi-Crop model.

At Nebraska, more records were broken. The 4050 was the quietest tractor ever, 70 dB(A) at 50 percent load and 73.5 dB at full.

From 1986, the 4050 had a turbo engine, giving it an extra 5 PTO hp.

Left: *This aerial photo of a 4450 illustrated the tight turns possible with Caster/Action MFWD.*

Below: *4850, number 13514, at work near Phoenix, Arizona, in January 1990. Deere had held its largest new product announcement that year in Palm Springs, California.*

Bottom left: *The Hi-Crop 4250 boasted a 30.3-inch (75-cm) crop clearance.*

Bottom right: *Ertl's replica of the largest 4850-MFWD on twin rears.*

2150, 2350, 2550, 2750, and 2950; 2255, 1982–1986

The smaller, Mannheim-built models and their PTO power ratings were the 45-hp 2150, 55-hp 2350, 65-hp 2550, 75-hp 2750, and 85-hp 2950. They had a new top-shaft-synchronized transmission (TSS) as standard; again with on-the-go shifting, this time within the gear ranges, saving time and giving efficient fuel use.

The 2150 through 2950 open-station versions were announced as Price Fighter models, which was of particular interest during the 1980s farming depression. The deluxe all-purpose models were offered with the Sound-Gard body option, the first time on the 55- to 75-hp models in the United States.

Speciality models included the orchard/vineyard 50-hp 2255, while the 2150, 2350, and 2550 could be equipped as low (for orchards), or narrow (for vineyards) models; the 2350 through 2950 with extra-wide 96-inch (240-cm) axles; and the 2750 as either a low-profile or hi-clearance (Mudder) tractor.

The 1984 series brochure covered the 2150 to 2950, as well as the 50-hp 2255 Orchard and Vineyard models and the 2750 High-Clearance (Mudder) and Low-Profile models.

A 2550's lights shine on a murky day. Note the 12-degree lean of the Caster/Action of the front-wheel-drive option.

Right: *The Hi-Crop, Low-Profile, Narrow- and Wide-Tread versions of the 50 Series justified their own brochure in 1985.*

Above: *The introductory brochure for the 50 Series models proclaimed them "Efficiency Experts."*

Left, top: *Ertl's 1/16-scale replica of the 2550-MFWD.*

Left, bottom: *John Westerveld's 1/32-scale 2750 Price Fighter replica.*

In Mexico, this 2755 Turbo Synchron model had the TSS transmission and MFWD.

2555, 2755, 4255, and 4455 Mexico, 1983–1993

In Mexico, Deere retained its own style of flat-top fenders when it introduced its new 55 Series models in 1983, built in the new premises in Saltillo acquired from International Harvester.

The 72-hp 2555 was offered in standard or orchard form, while the more powerful 82-hp 2755 was offered in four styles: standard with turbo 239-ci (3,915-cc) engine or Turbo Synchron with TSS transmission; orchard; or Hi-Crop, similar to the U.S. Mudder. All except the Hi-Crop could be two-wheel or MFWD; MFWD was standard on the Hi-Crop.

For larger farms the 140-hp 4255 and 153-hp 4455 were imported from the United States. All models were open station with optional two-post Roll-Gard on the two smaller sizes and four-post on the two larger.

John Westerveld's replica of the Waterloo-built two-wheel-drive 4255 with four-post ROPS and canopy as it was imported into Mexico.

80B Series Australia, 1984–1985

The Australian 80B Series had minor modifications from the 80 Series, which had been the first full series with Deere engine and design features. The linkage versions on the new series had extending lower links as on the U.S. models, an extending drawbar, and different decals, giving a more up-to-date look.

In addition, the 4080B was now the only row-crop model; in the first series, both the 3380 and 4080 were available with adjustable front axle; they were also supplied with six-post Roll-Gard in place of the "sedan," or cab. The row-crop tractors were called Cane models in Australia.

The 1983 brochure of the 80B Series had the leader of the line, the 4480B, working under lights with a Chamberlain drill.

The second Australian series after Deere acquired the company were the 80B models. The most powerful model of the new series was the six-cylinder 119-hp 4480.

90 Series Australia, 1985–1986

The last tractors to be built in Welshpool were the 90 Series, still with Chamberlain decals, but now painted green and yellow. They were available with Caster/Action MFWD as well as standard two-wheel format, and more closely resembled the Waterloo models in styling. The new cab was also similar to the U.S. Sound-Gard though more angular, and was complete with Personal-Posture seat, tilt-telescope steering wheel, and a 15-liter cooler as standard.

All models now had six-cylinder engines, 359 ci (5,880 cc) on the two smaller, 466 ci (7,633 cc) on the two larger, and turbocharged on the three larger, with power from 101 to 164 hp, or 94 to 154 PTO hp. All could have optional three-point linkage and adjustable front axles on two-wheel drives. The linkage was Category 2 on the 4090 and 4290, Category 3 and 3N on the 4490 and 4690.

Transmissions were 12/4 collar shift with hydraulic Hi-Lo. Independent hydraulic PTO on the two smaller models was 540 rpm standard, 1,000 rpm optional; the two larger models had 1,000 rpm only.

All four models represented the latest thinking for the mid-1980s in design and performance.

Below: *The May 1985 90 Series brochure gave a full description of the four models, although they only remained in production until the following year.*

Above: *The 4090 replaced the 3380B. It had a six-cylinder engine like the rest of the 90 Series, but was the only naturally aspirated model. All four models could have the MFWD option, adjustable front axles on the two-wheel-drive models, and three-point linkage.*

Right: *John Westerveld's model of the 4290-MFWD with twin rears.*

2155, 2355N, and 2555, 1987–1992

Deere's 150th anniversary arrived in 1987, and the complete line of Mannheim- and Getafe-built models were revised. For the U.S. market the smaller tractors became the 55 Series. The 2155 had a three-cylinder, 179-ci (2,932-cc) engine; the narrow 2355N orchard/vineyard model had a similar-sized three-cylinder turbo, the first on the U.S. market.

The 2555 could have either a naturally aspirated engine or, if fitted with the TSS transmission, a turbo version of the same 239-ci (3,915-cc) engine.

The speciality models, including those supplied for industrial use in the smart yellow and black finish, were usually open-station versions with Roll-Gard. All models could have the Sound-Gard body.

Below: *A new open-station 2555-MFWD at Goodrich Equipment Company of Geneseo, Illinois, in 1989. Note the new-type curved-end exhaust pipe instead of a rain cap.*

Above: *To celebrate Deere's 150th anniversary, the firm had a 2155, 4450, and 8650 on show outside the Administrative Center in 1987.*

Left: *Brochure showing the Utility 53-hp 2155 and 64-hp 2355 covering both green farm and yellow industrial models.*

2755, 2855N, and 2955, 1987–1992; 3155, 1988–1991

The larger tractors from Mannheim and Getafe were also updated in 1987. Both the 2755 and the 2855N orchard/vineyard models had turbo four-cylinder, 239-ci (3,915-cc) engines. The 2955 retained the 2950's six-cylinder, 2,300-rpm, 359-ci (5,880-cc) engine, which showed a slight increase in both PTO and drawbar power at Nebraska.

All the 55 Series were introduced as the Task Masters, and they certainly covered all the many tasks set to tractors in the 45- to 85-PTO-hp range. Both the 2755 and 2955 could be supplied as high-clearance models for veg-

etable growers or muddy fields; hence the name Mudder. The 2755 was supplied with two-post Roll-Gard as standard, with a canopy optional. The 2955 could have a Sound-Gard cab, four-post ROPS with canopy, or two-post ROPS with or without canopy.

The Mudders both featured a twelve-speed synchronized creeper transmission with a low speed of 0.27 mph (0.4 kph) for the 2755 and 0.33 mph (0.5 kph) for the 2955. The engaging clutch on MFWD models and the PTO clutch on all models were oil cooled, neither needing adjustment, and ensuring long life. This also applied to the brakes.

In 1988, the 95-hp 3155 was added to the line, with its rated engine speed increased to 2,400 rpm.

The largest six-cylinder model from Mannheim in 1991 was this 3155-MFWD. It is pictured alongside the beautifully restored Model 110, number 2991, owned by Klug Farm Equipment of Eau Claire, Michigan, USA.

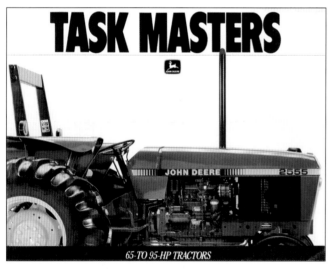

The general brochure covering the 2555 to 3155 Task Masters.

The Ertl replica of the agricultural 2755 with MFWD and SG2 cab.

1350, 1550, 1750, and 1850, 1987–1993; 1950, 1988–1993

In Europe, the 50 Series from both Mannheim and Getafe was announced for 1987 at the same time as the 55 Series in the United States. As before, there were several additional models to cover the requirements of small farmers in a variety of areas.

There were four three-cylinder models with the 179-ci (2,932-cc) engine: the 38-hp 1350, 44-hp 1550, 50-hp 1750, and 56-hp 1850. The turbo three-cylinder 62-hp 1950 was added to the line in 1988; the U.S. 2355N orchard/vineyard model used the same engine.

As well as more small models, an extra cab was introduced for work in low barns. This replaced the earlier low-style OPU and was called the MC1. It was available for all the three-cylinder models except the 1350, which was supplied with a safety frame only.

Right, top: *The CC2 safety cab replaced the earlier MC1 model, and was supplied for use in low buildings, usually on stock farms.*

Right: *The 1750V was available in two- or four-wheel-drive form, and was unique in having its headlights inserted in the nose of the hood. It also had the fuel tank behind its seat.*

Experience a surprising new level of comfort, convenience and control in an economical cab.

A standard 1850-MFWD with MC1 safety cab making its way homeward.

2250, 2450, 2650, and 2850, 1987–1993

The four- and six-cylinder models had their U.S. counterparts. The four four-cylinder models in Europe had both two-wheel and MFWD options, and MC1 or SG2 cab options. The models were the 62-hp 2250 (similar in power to the largest three-cylinder turbo 1950), the 70-hp 2450, 78-hp 2650, and 86-hp 2850. The MFWD option was becoming increasingly popular.

In 1990, another low-style cab was introduced, the CC2, replacing the MC1, with doors on both sides, a clear deck, and tiltable steering column as in the SG2, improving access. It was available for three- and four-cylinder models.

Above, top: *An overhead view of a 2450-MFWD with SG2 cab and 550 baler in the straw harvest.*

Above, left: *The May 1995 brochure for the 2250 to 2850 four-cylinder European models featured the 2850-MFWD plowing stubble with a two-way plow.*

Above, right: *This 2250-MFWD was fitted with a MC1 cab. It was photographed at the Parsons Bros. Deere dealership of Birdlip, near Gloucester, England.*

3050, 3350, and 3650, 1987–1993; 4350, 1985–1993

There were three six-cylinder 50 Series models all fitted with the 359-ci (5,880-cc) engine: the 3050 and 3350 engines were naturally aspirated, the 3650 was turbo. The first two had eight-speed TSS transmissions, while the 3650 had a sixteen-speed TSS with MFWD as standard, like its predecessor the 3640. A low-roof-style SG2 was an option on the six-cylinder models. The last 3650 built, 775621, was delivered to a dealer in Pembroke, South Wales, in February 1994.

The 4350 replaced the 4240S in 1985 and remained in the line to the end of the 50 Series. It was assembled from Waterloo units, and had a six-cylinder turbo 140-hp engine, making it the top of the European line.

Right, top: A new 3350-MFWD stands beside an earlier, used 3140 2WD. Note the new- and old-type exhaust pipes.

Right: The Ertl 1/32-scale 3650-MFWD model complete with operator.

Below: The 4350-MFWD replaced the 4240S-MFWD model in 1985. It was built in Mannheim from Waterloo assemblies.

A two-wheel-drive 2650 with CC2 cab spraying in a South Dakota orchard. Note the extended black engine guards that were fitted to all 50 Series tractors except the vineyard models.

Getafe 1750V, 1850, 1950, 2250, 2450, 2650, 2850, 3150, and 3350, 1987–1993

Getafe now produced the specialist models in addition to some standard models. On March 10, 1987, the 150,000th tractor built there was a 2450S-DT (standard model with MFWD) fitted with an SG2 Sound-Gard cab.

The specialist models were available in four styles: standard (S), vineyard (V), orchard (F), and multi- or high-crop (M); the S, V, and F models with MFWD were referred to as *Doble Traccion* (DT). The 1750V was vineyard only; the 1850 was offered in all six versions; the 1950 as S or F, both with DT option; the four-cylinder 2250 in S, S-DT, or M; the 2450 in S, F, and M, with DT on the first two; the 2650 in S and F; and the 2850, 3150, and 3350 in standard only, all four with optional DT (MFWD).

Just to complicate matters further, the orchard models sold in France were called the 1950N and 2650N using the American N letter designation. They also had different shell-type fenders and lighting positions.

The Getafe brochure for the orchard models covered the three- and four-cylinder tractors, including the 1850 and 1950 with normal and the 2450 and 2650 with turbo engines. The 1850FG had the 540/1000-rpm PTO option of the larger models.

This Spanish brochure illustrated the Euro four-wheel-drive series. The 37-hp 42AW and 42-hp 50A were on larger wheels than the 8.25x16-inch (20.625x40-cm) that were standard on the 42BW and 50B models.

Goldoni, 1987–1997

The sesquicentennial year saw another interesting development in Europe. Deere arranged with Goldoni of Italy to market a number of Goldoni models, initially in Spain. They were fitted with Deere engines supplied from Saran, and their styling was brought in line with other Deere models.

There were three orchard models: the 42-hp 445, 49-hp 604, and 60-hp 614. These were soon replaced with four models: the 1445 with the same engine as the 445, the 48-hp 1745, 56-hp 1845, and 67-hp 2345. Some of these were available in other European markets as well as Spain.

In addition to the orchard models, a number of smaller tractors were adopted and adapted with engines from 21 to 42 hp, or 17.7 to 38 PTO hp. There were four rigid-frame, four-equal-sized-wheel models, the 933, 938, 1038, and 1042; and three with articulated frames, the 921, 933, and U238. The last two digits indicated the engine horsepower. In 1993, only the largest rigid-frame 1042 was left in the line, while the articulated models had been updated to the 42-hp EURO 42 and a larger EURO 50 with a 50-hp engine.

All of the Goldoni models were similarly styled. Goldoni also built two-wheel tractors for terrace work, which Deere did not market.

John Westerveld built this 2345F Goldoni model.

The three original Italian models were replaced with four new versions: the 42-hp 1445F, 48-hp 1745F shown here, a new 56- hp model 1845F, and the 67-hp 2345F.

Above, top: *The standard, open-station, two-wheel-drive 2251 set the scene for the South African 51 Series styling. Note the position of the dismountable toolbox.*

Above, bottom: *The 51 Series brochure featured the 3651, 2651, 2351, and 3351, all with MFWD.*

2251, 2351, 2651, 2951, 3351, and 3651 South Africa, 1987–1993

In South Africa, the five-size, twelve-model 41 Series was replaced with the six-size, thirteen-model 51 Series in 1987. The ten four-cylinder, 236-ci (3,866-cc) ADE-engined models were: 2251 and 2251N (orchard) with two-wheel drive (TWD in South Africa) or MFWD; 2351, 2651, and 2951T with similar options. The 2351 and 2651 were altitude compensated, the 2951 was turbo.

The operator's platform on the four-cylinder tractors was redesigned to give easier access. The chassis on all models was strengthened with an increased front axle oscillation from 9 to 12 degrees for both TWD and MFWD models.

The two six-cylinder models had 354-ci (5,799-cc) ADE engines, both altitude compensated; the 3351 was offered in both TWD and MFWD form; the 3651 with MFWD only. A two-post Roll-Gard with canopy was standard on these two models, optional on the four smaller.

The independent PTO was 540 rpm on the two smaller sizes, 540/1,000 rpm interchangeable on the four larger. Differential lock was standard on all, with an eight-speed TSS transmission on the 2251 and 2351; sixteen-speed TSS on the 2651 to 3651.

2850, 3350, and 3550 Argentina, 1988–1993

For 1988, Rosario streamlined its operation and produced just three 50 Series models: the 95-hp four-cylinder turbo 2850 in two-wheel-drive form only; and two six-cylinder models, the 110-hp naturally aspirated 3350 with optional two-wheel drive or MFWD, and the turbo 125-hp 3550 with MFWD standard. The 4450 MFWD was imported from Waterloo for the largest farmers. All three models followed Mannheim equivalents with the open station and flat-top fenders of the series they replaced.

Above, top: *MFWD was standard on the leader of the line, the 125-hp 3550. Its engine was the same size as the 3350 but was turbo.*

Above, bottom: *John Westerveld's 3550 replica of the Argentine 50 Series.*

A new 8760 on twin tires at Klug Farm Equipment of Eau Claire, Michigan, in 1991.

Thirty year of progress is represented here: the latest 8960 370-engine-hp tractor on triple tires alongside the 1960s 215-hp 8020 with single wheels, which was considered a giant in its day.

Above: *Ertl 1/16-scale 8760 on twins.*

Right: *August 1988 brochure of the 60 Series four-wheel-drive tractors shows their new styling, with muffler and air intake removed to the corner of the cab. It covered the three models: the 235-hp 8560, 300-hp 8760, and 370-hp 8960.*

8560, 8760, and 8960, 1988–1992

The articulated four-wheel-drive models were completely redesigned in 1988. The new 60 Series was announced in the fall, in Denver, and joined the 55 Series of two-wheel tractors in January 1989 at the company's largest product announcement to date, in Palm Springs.

Completely new from the ground up, the three models were the 8560 with a 7.6-liter engine of 235 hp and 200 PTO hp; the 8760 with a 10.1-liter engine of 300 hp and 256 PTO hp; and the 8960 with a 14-liter Cummins engine giving 370 hp and 322 PTO hp. The six-cylinder, 1,900-rpm, 14-liter Cummins engine replaced the V-8 of the 8850, since the production costs did not justify its continuance.

The transmission options were twelve-speed Synchro or twenty-four-speed PowrSync with built-in Hi-Lo for all three models, or twelve-speed Power Shift for the two larger. The new Sound-Gard body had a full-width, one-piece upper windshield, side-opening door, stair step for easier access, and more room for the operator.

With three new engines, three new transmissions, an all-new chassis with center-frame oscillation, and a new Sound-Gard body designed specifically for these tractors, the three models represented the ultimate in four-wheel-drive tractors in 1988.

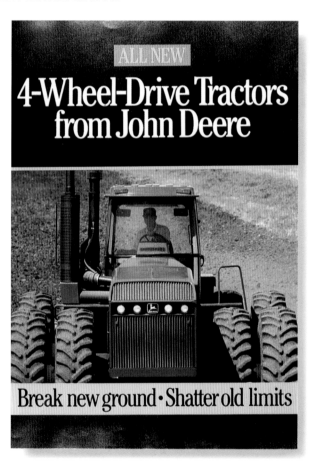

4055, 4255, and 4455, 1989–1992; 4555, 4755, and 4955, 1989–1991

At the 1989 Palm Springs new product announcement, the new Waterloo 55 Series debuted with six models in place of the five of the 50 Series they replaced. There were three narrow-frame models—the 4055, 4255, and 4455—and three wide-frame—the 4555, 4755, and 4955; the six ranged in power from 105 to 200 PTO hp. The two frame sizes were easily recognized, as the narrow models had three headlights in the grille; the wider ones had four.

New features included an MFWD now engaged automatically; a new IntelliTrak monitoring system; new cab comfort features; and electrohydraulic hitch control on the three larger models. The 4255 Hi-Crop replaced the 4250 model.

The three larger row-crop models included the new-size 4555 with 155 PTO hp, 175-hp 4755, and 200-hp 4955. The 4955 was thus the first row-crop tractor to have 200 hp available at its PTO. All three models had the turbo 7.6-liter engine rated at 2,200 rpm;the 4755 and 4955 boasted aftercoolers.

The Ertl replica of the 4455-MFWD.

4055-MFWD, number 1461. Owner: Ripon Farm Services, Ltd., of York, England.

A 4255HC Hi-Crop.

Ertl's replica of the wide-frame 55 Series 4955-MFWD.

Above: *Announcement of the 55 Waterloo Series in Europe was made at the Salon de la Machine Agricole at Port de Versailles in Paris, France, in March 1989.*

Right: *As the 4555 was not exported to Europe, the Mannheim brochure only showed the 4755 and 4955.*

3055 and 3255, 1991–1992

In 1991, the 3155 was replaced by two six-cylinder models from Mannheim, the naturally aspirated 92-hp 3055 and the turbo 100-hp 3255.

Open-station models were still standard with foldable Roll-Gard ROPS and seat belt, while a four-post version with canopy or the SG2 Sound-Gard body were other options. Rack-and-pinion rear axles, front rubber fenders for MFWD models, a hammer-stop drawbar, and a radio for open-station models were among the many options obtainable for all the larger 55 Series tractors.

Studio view of the 3255-MFWD with SG2 cab.

The two-wheel-drive 92-hp 3055 and four-wheel-drive 100-hp 3255, which replaced the 95-hp 3155-MFWD.

455, 655, 755, 855, and 955, 1986–1998; 670, 770, 870, 970, and 1070, 1989–1998

Originally announced in 1986, the 55 Series of under-40-hp hydrostatic-drive compact tractors included the 655, 755, and 855, all with optional MFWD. In 1989, the 33-hp 955 arrived with standard MFWD. All these models had three-cylinder diesel engines, 540-rpm PTO, and Category 1 three-point hitch. In 1990, the 655 was dropped, but in 1993 a new model, the 455, was introduced.

For customers who preferred gear-driven tractors, a new line was introduced in 1989. The 70 Series was built by Yanmar. The three new models from the 18.5-hp 670 to the 28-hp 870 had three-cylinder diesel engines; the two larger models, the 33-hp 970 and 38.5-hp 1070, were four-cylinder. The series replaced the 650 through 1050 line, which had also been built by Yanmar. Although chiefly geared to the grounds care market, the larger models were ideal for small farmers, especially when fitted with the 80 front loader and hitch-mounted implements.

All Deere implements designed for the earlier 50 Series could be fitted to or used with the 55 and 70 Series.

Right: *This brochure covered both the 70 Series models and the 55 Utility models.*

Below: *The 55 and 70 Series models on show. Owner: Frank Sutton of Raglan, Gwent, Wales.*

Above: *The 1070-MFWD with 80 front loader was capable of a man-size job.*

Left: *A 755 with cab at the Langar company branch house for the United Kingdom and Eire.*

4560, 4760, and 4960, 1991–1993

The three larger Waterloo row-crop tractors were again upgraded in 1991 to the 60 Series. The engines were the same as in the 55 Series they replaced, but many detail improvements were made at customers' requests. The new models adopted the articulated models' exhaust and air intake routing by the cab corner, improving the operator's view over the hood. At the same time, access to the new Sound-Gard body was greatly improved, with wider steps, a spacious platform that could be rotated 20 degrees to match row-crops or mounted tools, and two support rails.

The fenders, with new non-glare lights, were restyled. Both oil and air filters were redesigned for easier and cleaner servicing. Although renumbered for the U.S. market, they retained their 55 Series numbers in Europe for their brief two years in production.

Left, center: *Ertl's 1/16-scale replica of the Waterloo 60 Series tractors.*

Left, bottom: *A twin-rear 4960-MFWD was featured on the cover of the full brochure.*

On twins, this 4760-MFWD was working a typical Midwest farm with a set of 630 disk harrows.

8570, 8770, 8870, and 8970, 1993–1996

Another twin-wheel 8570, this time drilling grain with a 787 air drill.

The final development before the company's next giant step was the introduction of the 70 Series 4WD models. Introduced as the Power-Plus tractors in 1993, the engine was increased from 235 to 250 hp in the 8570; the 8770 retained the 8760's 300-hp engine; an extra tractor, the 8870, had an uprated 10.1-liter engine giving 350 hp; and the top-of-the-range 8970 was the first Deere with 400 hp. They all had electronic engine control, and for the first time, the three larger could be fitted with triple wheels all around.

Economic twelve-speed Synchro was standard on all four models, with twenty-four-speed PowrSync as an option, but twelve-speed Power Shift was only offered on the three larger. A 1,000-rpm PTO was optional on all four models.

Above: *The 8570 on twins with twin-axle 550 grain cart helping with the harvest.*

Left: *The 1993 70 Series brochure.*

CHAPTER 8

The World's Leader, 1991–1999

Above: *"Sign of the Right Choice"*: 8000/8000T brochure.

Left: *Model 6900 with Claas quadrant baler. (Photograph © Andrew Morland)*

NOUVEAUX TRACTEURS SÉRIE 2000 DE 89 À 106 CH (66 À 79 KW)

A French brochure of the 2800-MFWD with cab.

A 2700-MFWD at the Mannheim works in 1995.

The rear cab window also can be locked open to improve ventilation. A two-speed rear wiper is standard equipment.

Both cab and open-station models feature noise- and vibration-dampening isolation mounts that smooth out bumps and reduce in-cab noise levels to less than 81.5 dB(A).

2000 Series, 1993–

Deere has a long history of acquiring other tractor makers, and in the 1990s, Big Green joined forces with Zetor of the Czech Republic, Renault in France, Carraro and Goldoni in Italy, and SLC in Brazil. Under these agreements, Deere sought to produce models required in different countries at competitive prices. The move also created extended markets for the Deere Power Systems (DPS) group and the engine works in Waterloo and Dubuque; Saran, France; Rosario, Argentina; and Torreón, Mexico.

In late 1993, Deere announced an agreement with Zetor to market Zetor models as a low-price line in certain countries. Called the 2000 Series, it included the three-cylinder, 49-hp 2000; and four four-cylinder models, the 62-hp 2100, the 68-hp 2200, the 74-hp 2300, and the turbo 81-hp 2400. Larger, turbo models of a different design included the 89-hp 2700, 100-hp 2800, and top-of-the-line 106-hp 2900.

All models were offered as open station with ROPS or with safety cab, and as two-wheel drive or MFWD. The five smaller tractors had 10/2 gearboxes standard; 10/10 gearboxes with a direction reverser was optional. The three larger had an 8/8 synchronized transmission with a reverser as standard; 16/4 with power Hi-Lo was an option. Hydrostatic steering and hydraulically operated disc brakes were standard on all models; wet-disc on the three larger. With its green-and-yellow finish and modern cab style, the 2000 Series was accepted in many areas, including Argentina, Mexico, Australia, and South Africa.

This view from above the 2000 Series cab shows the access from both sides and the tidy layout.

3000, 3000X, and 3000SE Series, 1993–1998

In late 1993, Deere began marketing tractors from the French firm Renault that were fitted with Deere engines from Saran. The 3000 Series included four basic models: the 55-hp, three-cylinder 3100; and three four-cylinder models, the 65-hp 3200, 75-hp 3300, and 85-hp turbo 3400. The latter three were also available as 3000X models. These featured a digital display dashboard, console-mounted controls, hydraulically assisted PTO, and a Comfort X cab. All cabs had two-door entry; the deluxe models were below 78 dB. All had a high-capacity heating, cooling, and air-circulating system, four powerful work lights, and a large tool box standard; a passenger seat was optional.

The choice of four fully synchronized transmissions met all requirements. The 10/10 was standard with a left-hand reverse lever, with all speeds the same in forward or reverse. A 20/20 box had a mechanical splitter requiring clutch operation, but gave a 22-percent torque increase.

The base gearbox could have an optional creeper range added to the splitter version for ten extra speeds from 0.25 to 1.3 mph (0.4–2.1 kph). Finally, the electrically controlled Twinshift Power Hi-Lo was ideal for those with a lot of haulage duties.

Two-wheel or MFWD with 55-degree steering angle and 6-degree caster angle on all models, a Deere exclusive, ensured short turns. There was a choice of three PTOs on the two smaller models—540, 540/540E, and 1,000 rpm—and the two latter on the 3300 and 3400 models. Differential lock was standard on all models.

For 1996, the 3300, 3300X, 3400, and 3400X were added in economy version at about 10 percent lower cost and called the SE or XSE Series.

In fall 1998, the 3000 and 3000 SE Series were brought into line with the medium-sized models and updated as the 3010 and 3010 SE Series. These new models featured some ten changes from the earlier models, including a brighter cab interior, new seat, frameless glass doors, and a 13-percent increase in lift capacity of the top two models.

The brochure covering the new 3000 Series showed an 85-hp 3400X-MFWD at plow.

Smallest of the 3000 Series built by Renault was the three-cylinder, 55-hp, two-wheel-drive 3100 with mounted grain and fertilizer drill.

Representing the 3000 Series, this 3400X-MFWD had the front PTO and hitch; it was in charge of a 570 French-factory-built large round baler.

Siku's 1/32-scale replica of the 3000 Series had both MFWD and cab.

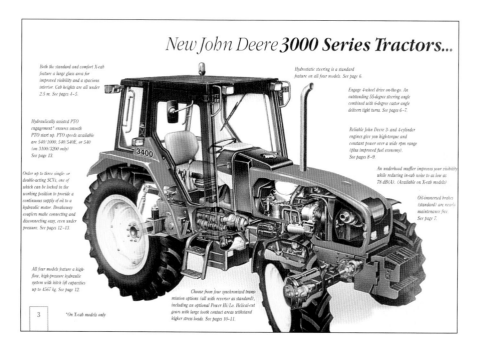

Cutaway section of the 3400X-MFWD.

A field view of the 3300X-SE economy model, which was introduced in 1996 due to the poor economy prevailing on European farms.

The 100-hp 4450, the middle of the three telescopic loader line, was made for pallet handling. The 4350 had a 92-hp four-cylinder turbo PowerTech engine; the 4450 and 4550 had similar 100-hp engines, the latter model having greater lift, height, and reach capacity.

4000 Series, 1997–

Arriving in 1997, Deere's new compact utility 4100 tractor was targeted at the under-20-hp market and priced to match the competition. With styling similar to the 5000 Ten Series, it was fitted with a new clean and silent three-cylinder Yanmar TNE diesel engine with high torque reserve; the 4100 Gear was offered with an 8/4 collar-shift gearbox, and the 4100 HST had a hydrostatic transmission. The 4000 Series replaced the gear-driven 670 and hydrostatic-drive 755, the two smallest models in each series.

Hydrostatic power steering, 2,100-rpm mid-PTO and 540-rpm rear PTO, open-center hydraulic system, and engage-on-the-go MFWD were all standard equipment. Operator safety was highlighted with PTO engagement light, brakes on both mid and rear PTO (HST), mid-PTO only (gear), and Hydro Drive safety shutdown. A new front loader, the 410, was designed for quick installation, and many other implements were interchangeable with 55 and 70 Series models.

During 1998, five more models were added to the 4000 Series compact utility line: the three-cylinder 21.5-PTO-hp 4200, 27-hp 4300, and 30-hp 4400; and the four-cylinder 33-hp 4500 and 36-hp 4600. Independent 540-rpm PTO was standard on all models, with mid-PTO and four-wheel drive optional. Tilt steering wheels, Roll-Gard ROPS, and seatbelts were also standard.

The extended 4000 Series replaced the gear-driven 70 Series and hydrostatic-drive 55 Series.

The July 1996 brochure introduced the new breed of sprayer for the large operator; as seen here, it could be a cross between a Wide-Axle and a Hi-Crop model tractor.

4100 Gear in a typical Midwestern setting.

4100 Compact earning its keep with a 410 front loader. This 4100 had four-wheel drive, ROPS, and a balancing weight tray.

Ertl's 1/16-scale 5200-MFWD.

5000 Series U.S., 1991–1997

Similar to the 1959 introduction of the 8010, the first of the new Thousand Series tractors, the 5000, was announced in late 1991 to be built in a new, purpose-constructed works in Augusta, Georgia. Bearing little recognizable connection with previous models but with Deere styling and colors, the 5000 had a totally new design concept.

Initially built as open-station models, operators had access to the clear platform from both sides, made possible by console-mounted controls, a further-forward position for the operator, and a fuel tank mounted behind the seat. The ROPS was foldable for orchard or low-barn work, hydrostatic power steering was standard, and MFWD was optional.

Using a 179-ci (2,932-cc), three-cylinder engine, the 5200 had 40 PTO hp; the 5300, 50 hp; and the 5400, 60 hp. In 1994, a narrow 5400N was announced.

Above: *The only 5000 Series tractor in the United Kingdom for some time was this 5200, imported from Canada by John Dorrell of Pershore, Worcestershire, England, for his own custom use.*

Right: *The July 1994 5000 Series brochure had a two-wheel-drive 5300 with 520 loader as its frontispiece.*

5500 Series, 1995–1997

In 1995, the line was extended by the four-cylinder 5500 and 5500N with 239-ci (3,915-cc) engines. In 1996, a new cab had entry from either side and air conditioning. The narrow or orchard/vineyard models had their own narrow-cab option.

This fully equipped 5400-MFWD had a front hitch and PTO plus a cab, showing the open front, side and rear windows. All windows and doors have locks.

An October 1996 brochure covering the 5300 and 5400 in normal trim.

5000 Series European, 1996–

In 1996, Deere arranged with Carraro in Rovigo, Italy, to produce certain 5000 Series models for Europe. Carraro began building the 5300 and 5400 standards and the 5300N, 5400N, and 5500N narrow models, all as two- or four-wheel drives. The line was further extended in November 1998 by the addition of the 80-hp 5500 standard model with both wheel arrangements.

In Europe, the N models had an optional special cab, though they were normally supplied with foldable ROPS; these could remain fixed to the cab-equipped tractor. It was only a ten-minute job to remove the cab if one had a tractor with loader to lift it. Another special feature of the N models was the special three-point linkage required to clear the rear wheels and was known as Category 1N.

The narrow models used in orchards and vineyards needed to be able to work with or without a cab. To remove the cab took ten minutes if you had a 6800 and 740A loader handy! Note the foldable ROPS still fixed and ready for action.

An April 1997 Spanish brochure for the three N models, 5300N, 5400N, and 5500N.

Laforge Greenlink front hitches for the 5000 to 8000 Series models were compatible with either the John Deere or Laforge front PTOs; they also fitted either two-wheel-drive or MFWD models. Their weight frame would carry the full complement of front weights.

The October 1997 brochure for the new 5000 Ten Series covered the three-cylinder 45-PTO-hp 5210 and 55-hp turbo 5310, the four-cylinder 65-hp 5410 and 75-hp turbo 5510, plus the 5310N and 5510N narrow tractors.

5010 Series, 1998–

Like the 7000 Series before it, the complete U.S. 5000 line was replaced in 1997 with the 5010 Series with increased power and added features for operator convenience. New features included PowerTech engines from 45 to 75 hp built in Deere's new Torreón engine factory; redesigned controls and instrumentation; optional 540/540E PTO with 9F/3R SyncShuttle gearbox, plus a 12F/12R Powr-Reverser transmission for shuttle work. ROPS or two-door cab with air conditioning were available.

The 5210 and 5310 had three-cylinder 3029 engines, whereas the 5410 joined the 5510 in boasting a new four-cylinder 4045 engine; the 5510 was turbo. Both have a 5.00-inch (127-mm) stroke instead of the previous 4.33-inch (110-mm) of the 5500. All models were governed at 2,400 rpm.

Overall dimensions of the Ten Series are similar to the previous models.

Right, top: *A fully equiped 5410 MFWD with cab and 540 front loader.*

Right, bottom: *A 5410 with cab. Note the entry from both sides.*

6000 Series, 1992–1997

In fall 1992, the next Thousand Series models were announced, the 6000 Series from Mannheim and the 7000 Series from Waterloo. Launched simultaneously in the United States and Europe, the 6000 Series initially consisted of four four-cylinder models: the naturally aspirated 75-hp 6100 for Europe; and the turbo 84-hp 6200, 90-hp 6300, and 100-hp 6400 for both markets.

The new tractors had an all-new modular design supported by a heavy-gauge independent steel main frame. Engine, transmissions, cab, steering, and electronically controlled hydraulics were all new, and few parts were interchangeable with earlier series. All models could have two-wheel drive or MFWD, and open-station or safety cabs; these latter were called ComfortGard in the United States, TechCenter in Europe. The safety cabs had two-door access resulting from their more forward position, achieved by moving the fuel tank below the platform. The SuperComfort seat, combined adjustment of command module and steering wheel, improved operator vision with the muffler moved to the cab corner and floor-to-roof glass, plus noise level of 72 dB made the 6000 Series the market trendsetter.

The 6000 open-station models also had steps on both sides, tilt steering wheel for easy access, foldable ROPS as standard, canopy optional, electronic monitors for all tractor functions, and an easy-to-read analog dash. The SuperComfort seat was optional. A 12/4 SynchroPlus transmission was standard for all four European models and on three U.S. models, with 15/5 and 18/6 options in Europe. A 16/12 PowerQuad was optional in the U.S. market, with 20/16 and 24/16 in Europe.

Other models available in the 6000 Series were the 6300 and 6400 High-Clearance versions with 38-inch (95-cm) front and 46-inch (115-cm) rear wheels; extra-wide models with up to 96-inch (240-cm) wheel spacing. The 6000L Series included the 6200L, 6300L, and 6400L with two- or four-wheel drive, and open station or cab. An orchard/vineyard 6000L Series of four models was also offered. The 6500L with 95 PTO hp was only available in orchard/vineyard configuration.

Late in 1993, two six-cylinder turbo models were added for European and export markets, replacing the much-liked 3350 and 3650. The 6600 had a 100-hp, six-cylinder version of the engine in the 6200 and 6300; the 120-hp 6800 had the same bore and stroke as the 6400, but was rated at 2,100 rpm instead of the 2,300 of the five other models in this series. Both the 6600 and 6800 had MFWD as standard. Transmissions on these two models were PowrQuad with two variations for each model: 20/20 or 24/24 for the 6600; 16/12 or 20/12 for the 6800, plus creeper option on all four giving 12/12 extra speeds.

For 1994, a third six-cylinder model was added, the 130-hp 6900. Rated at 2,100 rpm like the 6800, its torque reserve was increased from 34 to 38 percent. Otherwise, all options were the same.

Both the 6600 and 6800 had MFWD standard. Transmissions on these two models were PowrQuad with two variations for each model: 20/20 or 24/24 for the 6600; 16/12 or 20/12 for the 6800, plus creeper option on all four giving 12/12 extra speeds.

For 1994, a third six-cylinder model was added, the 130-hp 6900. Rated at 2,100 rpm like the 6800, its torque reserve was increased from 34 to 38 percent. Otherwise, all options were the same. In 1995, a fourth six-cylinder model, the 105-hp 6506, joined the line with the same options as the 110-hp 6600.

6100-MFWD at Girvan, Scotland, in 1992.

Announcing the All-New Breed of Power, the first U.S. brochure in July 1992 covered the 6200 to 6400 and 7600 to 7800 models.

One of the first 6400 models imported to the United Kingdom was photographed outside the premises previously owned by the author.

The French brochure for the 6000 Series Highway models.

A 6800, number 118092, outside the premises of R. Tincknell & Son of Wilton, Wiltshire, England.

Spotted in the works at Mannheim in 1995, this 6300-MFWD Highway model was connected to a machine through its front PTO.

In August 1992, the 6000 Series acquired its own DKA105 brochure.

High-Clearance 6400 seen outside the Deere dealership in Ripon, California.

Introduced in 1995, the 6506 was the similarly powered six-cylinder equivalent of the four-cylinder 6400 but with a naturally aspirated engine.

This 6400L-MFWD had a new low-clearance cab. Built for orchards, groves, and confined spaces, this cab had a unique A-frame design.

SPECIAL DIMENSION TRACTORS
HIGH-CLEARANCE, ORCHARD/VINEYARD AND WIDE-ROW TRACTORS

New brochure for 1992 covering the High-Clearance 6300 and 6400, and the Wide-Row 6200 to 6400.

Ertl's replica of the 6200-MFWD with cab and front loader.

Ertl replica of the 6400-MFWD open-station model with ROPS.

Above: *6900 with five-furrow, two-way plow in heavy land in 1996. Owner: Rosie Barber, Newham Hall, Northumberland, England.*

Left: *6800, number 118092, at the Deere branch of R. Tincknell & Son of Wilton, Wiltshire, England.*

Left, bottom: *The six-cylinder 6000 Series brochure had a twin-wheel all-around 6900 on its cover.*

A 6200SE-MFWD operating a PTO-driven unit popular in Europe.

6000 SE Series, 1996–1997

The low-cost 6200 SE and 6400 SE were announced in Europe in fall 1996 as the Task Masters. Advertised as simple, economical, and functional, they were the odd-job tractor at a reasonable price, which was about 10 percent below the standards. The 6200L SE and 6400L SE had low-profile cabs, and all four models had the SyncroPlus transmission standard, with Power Reverser optional.

The September 1996 brochure for 6000 SE models showed the 6200-MFWD SE tractor working with a combination cultivation-drilling unit. It also covered the 6400 SE model.

This 6200SE-MFWD was rotary cultivating and drilling in a combined operation.

6010 Series, 1998–

Announced at the DLG Show in Frankfurt, Germany, in November 1997, the 6010 Series had a range of innovative ideas in addition to increased power on all but the 6510, the replacement for the 6506. The new series were all fitted with the new generation of PowerTech 4.5- and 6.8-liter engines designed to meet future U.S. and European emission regulations likely to be introduced over the next five years. All 6010 Series models except the 6510 were turbocharged.

The unique feature of the new series was Triple Link Suspension (TLS) that stopped roadwork bounce. The front axles were supported by two hydraulic cylinders mounted vertically on the tractor frame front, and an axially mounted arm running from the axle to the frame's central casting. An optional electronic level control monitored and constantly centralized the axle suspension for models from the 6310 to 6910.

Eight different transmissions were available depending on the model: four PowrQuad versions, two new PowrQuad Plus, and two new AutoQuad versions. PowrQuad Plus provided push-button shifting using a single lever control, and was optional for all models. AutoQuad had the same features but incorporated electronic fuel injection governing, cruise control, and automatic gear shifting within the range; the transmission shifted automatically depending on engine rpm and load. All eight gearboxes could have a 12/12 creeper speed option.

The 6010 Series cab had four driver seat options, a suspended passenger seat, and extra storage space. For 6310 models up, the seat could be swiveled 180 degrees for forestry or backhoe work, and had a special active carbon layer to absorb moisture. Positioned further forward on the tractor, it provided wider access doors and 310 degree visibility; noise levels were further reduced. Other features included a Field Office storage compartment pre-wired for mobile phones and portable computers, automatic hitch dampening, rear PTO remote control, and the Headland Management System (HMS), allowing automatic disengagement of four-wheel drive, differential lock, and PTO when raising the three-point hitch. This gave easier headland turning, and when the hitch was lowered, it re-engaged the four-wheel drive and differential lock; the operator had to re-engage the PTO for safety reasons. The pick-up hitch was redesigned, new power brakes were proportionally actuated, and the front PTO was synchronized with the rear so that both reach the same speed at the same engine speed.

Clearing the ground after grain harvest, a 6410-MFWD loads big round bales with a 640A front loader.

The six-cylinder 6010 Series brochure covered the four models 6510 to 6910, which were not marketed in the United States because the two larger had equivalents in the 7210 and 7410. Its cover depicted the top-of-the-line 6910 with 420A mulch finisher.

Right: *A 6010 Series tractor with its TechCenter cab tilted for overhauls and upgrades. Brakes, steering, gear shift, and SCV cables all remained attached when the cab was tilted.*

Below: *Largest of the 6010 Series in Europe, a 140-hp 6910 with a local supplier's five-furrow, two-way plow.*

7000 Series, 1992–1996

At the same time that Mannheim announced the first 6000 models, Waterloo launched the 7000 Series. The three most powerful models were available in fall 1992 for the 1993 season: the 7600 with 130 engine hp, 110 PTO hp; 7700 150/125; and 7800 170/145. In 1993, the 92-PTO-hp 7200 and 100-PTO-hp 7400 were added, the U.S. equivalents of the 6600 and 6800. Again all five models could be 2WD or MFWD, open station or with the new cab.

All five 7000 Series were turbocharged with 2,100-rpm rated engines and a choice of three transmissions. The two smaller had twelve-speed SyncroPlus standard with 16/12 PowrQuad as optional; a further choice with PowrQuad was a 12/12 creeper with speeds from 0.10–0.98 mph (0.16–1.5 kph). The three larger models had the 16/12 PowrQuad standard with 12/12 creeper or nineteen-speed Power Shift optional. The open-station models had many features found on those with cabs. The access was from both sides, the platform was rubber mounted, and the steering wheel telescopic and tiltable to match with the personal-posture seat. The two-post ROPS was standard and foldable with a handy built-in lever to raise and lower it.

When the two smaller six-cylinder 7000 Series tractors were announced in 1993, Hi-Crop and High Clearance models were also added. The Hi-Crop had 40 inches (100 cm) clearance under the back axle, while the latter was about 30 inches (75 cm). Options included two- or four-wheel drive, and cab or open station, while the PTO, differential lock, and hydraulic system were the same for the whole series. The creeper option was particularly applicable to these models when working in vegetable crops and pick-and-pack operations. The high clearances were also ideal for tall crops and high beds.

Right, top: *An open-station 7600 baling straw, emphasizing the high operator's position on these models.*

Right, center: *Illustrating its adaptability, this top-of-the-line 7800 was mowing with a front-mounted PTO-driven 228 mower-conditioner and a rear-drawn 1360, both neatly laying their two windrows side by side.*

Above: *The 1992 U.S. brochure had the 7600 and 7700 two-wheel-drive models and the 7800-MFWD on the cover, all with ComfortGard cabs.*

Open-station 7200 Hi-Crop. The High-Clearance models had the smaller front wheels, and were really the Standard model on larger diameter wheels all around, while the Hi-Crop had rear drop axles. Both the Hi-Crop and High-Clearance had Caster/Action MFWD for short turns.

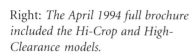
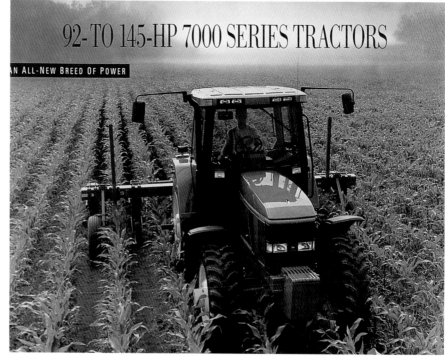

92-TO 145-HP 7000 SERIES TRACTORS

AN ALL-NEW BREED OF POWER

Right: *The April 1994 full brochure included the Hi-Crop and High-Clearance models.*

Below: *Ertl's replica of the 7800 four-wheel drive on twin rears.*

7010 Series, 1996–

First of the Thousand Series to be updated was the 92- to 145-PTO-hp 7000 Waterloo Series, which became the 7010, or 7000 Ten, Series in 1996 with increased power from new PowerTech engines. The 7210, 7410, and 7610 had six-cylinder 6068 engines built in Dubuque, while the 7710 and 7810 had Waterloo-built 6081 engines. The tractors could be ordered with or without cabs, with two-wheel drive or MFWD, and with a choice of three transmission options. The 7210 and 7410 were available as High-Clearance or Hi-Crop models, both with cab or open station. All models featured better ventilation and climate control in the cabbed versions, brighter lighting, and smoother shifting with the Powershift models. There was a new left-hand power reverser option for the PowrQuad transmission that provided no-clutch direction changes for loader work and the like.

There were four front loaders made for the series: the 720 and 725 for 2WD models, and the 740 and 740 Mechanical-Self-Leveling (MSL) for MFWD tractors. Many options were available to customize tractors, including front and rear weights, a rugged Quik-Coupler, foot throttle, front fenders for MFWD, outside mirrors for both sides of the cab, a rear windshield wiper, an air brake system for heavy trailers, and both radio and power strip harnesses.

This 7810 and trailer were coping with the output of one of the new 280/310-hp 6650 self-propelled forage harvesters.

First of the Thousand Series to be updated were the 7000 models in the United States. Shown here is a 7810-MFWD with 420A Mulch Tiller at a dealer presentation on the farm of Alec McKee near Nottingham, England.

Modern drilling methods are exemplified in this aerial photo of a 7810-MFWD at work with a 740A mulch drill

Ertl's replica of the top-of-the-line 7810-MFWD with cab.

At work cultivating, this 7810-MFWD had a Laforge front hitch designed to integrate with the factory-supplied front PTO.

The European brochure for the new series referred to them as 7010 Series, whereas the U.S version called them the 7000 Ten Series. The former only covered models 7610 to 7810, the latter 7210 to 7810 plus the 7210/7410 Hi-Crop and High-Clearance models.

SLC Brazil, 1996–

SLC–John Deere of Horizontina, Brazil, assembled models for the Mexican and South American markets, including the 5600, 5700, 6300, all available in either two-wheel drive or MFWD; the two-wheel drive 6500 for Argentina; and the 6600 and 7500 as MFWD only.

The 5600 had a four-cylinder 4039D naturally aspirated 75-hp engine; the 5700 and 6300 had 4039T 85- and 100-hp turbo engines; and the 6500 had a 6059D 115-hp naturally aspirated engine. All four engines were assembled in Saltillo, Mexico, with components from Saran. The six-cylinder 6600 had a 121-hp 6059T and the 7500 a 140-hp 6068T; both turbo engines came from Saran.

In addition to the SLC-assembled models, Argentina imported the 2300 and 2800 with Zetor engines; the 5400 assembled in Saltillo and similar to the original Augusta model; and the 8200 and 8300 from Waterloo.

Above: The April 1996 brochure issued by SLC–John Deere covered the 6000 and 7000 models, including the four-cylinder, two- and four-wheel-drive, 85-PTO-hp 6300, and the six-cylinder, four-wheel-drive, 103-hp 6600 and 119-hp 7500. All four models were turbo.

Left: Two- and four-wheel-drive turbo 2400 models as assembled in Mexico for the Mexican and South American market. The model was similar to the naturally aspirated 2300.

The Portuguese brochure showed the 946 at work with an integral John Deere rotary cultivator on the cover.

The turbo four-cylinder, two-wheel-drive 6400SP and four-wheel-drive 6400SP-DT open-station models were assembled in Saltillo and marketed in Mexico. They were the same as the Mannheim-built versions.

The 37- to 42-hp four-wheel-drive series from Goldoni were still marketed in Spain and Portugal as of 1998. The Euro 42AW illustrated had the larger, 18-inch (45-cm) wheels fitted to this model and the 50A.

46 and 46FA Series Spain and Portugal, 1996–

In 1996, the tractors from Goldoni were augmented by three new models, the 20-engine-hp 746, 28-hp 846, and 32-hp 946, all with three-cylinder diesel engines, MFWD, and 540/1,000-rpm PTO standard. Offered in Spain and Portugal, they were ideal tractors for orchard and vineyard work.

For 1998, the four larger orchard 45 Series Goldoni models were replaced by three new 46FA Series models, the 1546FA, 1846FA, and 2446FA. They had MFWD—*doble traccion* in Spanish—and a hydraulic differential lock as standard. Their complete platform/fender unit was rubber mounted, and the steering wheel was telescopic for operator comfort. They had three-cylinder PowerTech Saran-built engines, from the naturally aspirated 45-hp 1546FA and 57-hp 1846FA to the top of the line 71-hp 2446FA turbo. With an 8/8 transmission with speeds from 1 to 25 mph (1.6–40 kph), they fully covered the requirements of orchard growers in their power range.

The Spanish brochure for the 6010 Series four-cylinder models covering the 80-hp 6110 to the 105-hp 6410.

With front- and rear-mounted implements, twin wheels all around were required by this 105-hp 6510.

6005 and 7005 Advantage Series, 1997–

Announced in 1997 for the U.S. market, the three economical Advantage Series models were the 85- hp 6405, 95-hp 6605, and 105-hp 7405. The 6405 and 7405 could be ordered as High-Clearance models. They were all open-station versions of the similar deluxe Ten Series models with the same engines, full-frame chassis, clutch, ROPS, and axles. Differences were in the HydraVantage load-sensing hydraulic system with constant-flow pump, instrumentation, transmissions, and attachments. As on the Advantage Series, Deere loaders were commonly mated with specific tractor models to give greater compatibility.

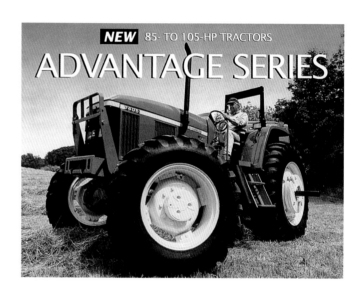

Above right: *The brochure covering the three Advantage models 6405, 6605, and 7405 was issued in July 1997. Its cover showed a 7405-MFWD with big baler in tow.*

Right: *Largest of the three Advantage models was the six-cylinder 7405-MFWD. All three models could be two- or four-wheel drive, and the 6405 and 7405 had High-Clearance options.*

8000 Series, 1994–

The introduction of the largest two-wheeled tractors in Deere's history offered twenty-first century technology in 1994. Everything about the 8000 Series was new: the CommandView cab with its increased visibility, CommandARM controls and instrumentation, exclusive Field Cruise control, and all-new 7.6- and 8.1-liter engines. The 225-PTO-hp 8400 was the largest two-wheeled tractor on the market and only available with MFWD. The other three models in the series—the 160-hp 8100, 180-hp 8200, and 200-hp 8300—could be equipped with either two-wheel drive or MFWD. Originally announced with 7.6-liter engines, the 8100, 8200, and 8300 were subsequently changed to the 8400's 8.1-liter Model 6081 turbo and aftercooled engine rated at 2,200 rpm.

The sight of an 8300-MFWD pulling a fourteen-bottom 14-inch (35-cm) plow was an awesome sight.

Left, top: *Ertl's 1/16-scale replica of the 8300-MFWD.*

Left: *The two largest members of the 8000 Series, the 200-hp 8300 and 225-hp 8400.*

Below: *8400-MFWD with a full complement of twenty European-style front weights, two extra headlamps, and mid-cab traffic indicators.*

A European 8000 Series model disking.

Above left: *The first full 8000 Series brochure was dated August 1994.*

Above right: *Ertl replica of the 8400-MFWD on twin rears.*

Left: *French brochure for the 8000 Series from December 1996.*

U.S. 8000T Series brochure emphasizing its inter-corn-row capabilities with a 16-inch (40-cm) belt.

Above: *John Westerveld's model of the 8400T.*

8000T Series, 1997–

Announced in 1996, the 8000T Series rubber-track models began production in June 1997. For the first time since the 10 Series of the 1960s, it was now possible to purchase either a wheeled or tracked version of the same tractor. Now, however, the tracks were rubber instead of steel link, and the model was the top of the line instead of the smallest.

Both the wheeled and track 8000T used the same engine and sixteen-speed Power Shift transmission, though the track model's speeds were lower—1.2 to 18.8 mph (1.92–30 kph) compared with 1.4 to 24 mph (2.24–38 kph) of the wheeled model. The extra wet-disk clutch for the MFWD was not required with the tracked machine.

Tracks were either 16 or 24 inches (40 or 60 cm) wide for row-crop work, with spacing adjustable from 60 to 88 inches (150 to 220 cm) in standard form. Deere listed the advantages of tires compared with tracks: Tires offered easy tread change, better transport ride quality, less cost, better turning under load, less vibration, less crop damage on headlands and in bedded rows, and faster transport speeds; tracks provided greater maneuverability, better ride in rough fields, better traction in loose soil and on steep hillsides, better flotation in wet fields, easier implement hookup, and minimal tire and ballast adjustment.

The CommandView cab with its Field Office and CommandArm controls were common to both types as were FieldCruise and TouchSet hydraulics. The track model did not have the 1⅜-inch 540/1,000-rpm PTO nor the Category 3N three-point hitch options. Otherwise, parts interchangeability was extensive.

For 1999, a wide-track version was added, with larger axles and a 30-inch (75-cm) track width.

Above: *The 8000T Series was introduced to the United Kingdom on September 4, 1997, with this 8400T with a 410A Mulch Tiller.*

Left: *The 8400T in U.S. trim with 16-inch (40-cm) belt width for row-crop work.*

9000 Series, 1996–

The largest tractor series built by Deere to date were the new 9000 four-wheel-drive models. Their engines were rated from 260 to 425 hp: The 9100 had the same 8.1-liter engine as the 8000 Series but rated at 2,100 rpm; the 9200 had a new 10.5-liter 6105 310-hp engine in place of the 10.1-liter used previously in the 8770 and 8870. The 360-hp 9300 and New World Power 425-hp 9400 had an all-new John Deere 12.5-liter PowerTech 6125 engine with four valves per cylinder, two-piece pistons, liners 17 percent thicker than the 10.1-liter, and electronically controlled fuel injectors. The 9400's camshaft alone weighed 72 pounds (32.4 kg). With its 7 percent power increase, the 9400 produced more than 450 hp at 1,900 rpm. With the models' 270 U.S. gallon (225 IMP) fuel tank capacity and increased fuel efficiency, one can budget on staying in the field for 20–25 percent longer without refuelling.

The engine hood on all models rose at the simple push of a button. Taking a lead from the 8000 Series, the new models had a CommandView cab with side-door entrance, CommandArm controls with the hitch, hydraulics, and throttle at your fingertips. The deluxe cab package included a multi-socket power strip, two interior mirrors, rear opening window, large seat drawer, and new field office—a desk, secretary, and storage cabinet in one.

Transmissions included the twelve-speed Syncro standard, with twenty-four-speed PowrSync optional on all four models; the three largest models could have the further option of a twelve-speed PowerShift. Three other options were a 1¾-inch 1,000 rpm PTO; a three-point hitch with Quick-Coupler, Category 3 on all, Category 4/4N optional on the two larger; and a power differential lock on both axles. Dual or triple radial tires could be ordered.

A nighttime photo of a 9400 with a 685 chisel plow, illustrating its comprehensive infrared lighting equipment.

The July 1996 brochure covered the new 9000 Series 260- to 425-hp tractors. The cover featured a 9300 on twins with a 650 disk working a hillside in undulating country.

Preparing a seedbed with a second pass, this 9200 had twin wheels all around.

Ertl's 1/16-scale model of the four-wheel-drive 9400 on twins.

9000T Series, 1999–

The 9300T was shown to the public for the first time at the Farm Progress Show in Windfall, Indiana, in fall 1998 as a concept tractor and test unit. It was a pre-production tracked version of the wheeled models that were due to go into production in 1999. Its configuration was similar to the smaller 8000T Series but with a four-roller track frame compared with the three-roller of the 8000T.

Its advent was looked forward to by farmers requiring the extra power of the 10.5-liter PowerTech 6105 and 12.5-liter 6125 engines, the latter with four valves per cylinder, two-piece pistons, liners 17 percent thicker than the old 10.1-liter engine, and electronically controlled fuel injectors.

Prototype for the new 9000T Series was this 8770 fitted with the four-roller track frame.

Below: *A pre-production 9300T with 1810 chisel plow.*

Into a New Millennium, 2000–

Above: *The Deere 8320RT, launched at the Berlin, Germany, presentation in August 2009.*

Left: *Old and new: the Deere 8530 alongside a Model D.*

In the spring of 2008, in a phone discussion with my editor, we considered the possibility of updating *The Big Book of John Deere Tractors*, since it was originally published in 2000. Much had happened at Deere & Company in the first decade of the twenty-first century.

Originally a sixteen-page addition was suggested, but a quick review of the Internet showed this would prove completely inadequate, and we agreed a whole new Chapter 9 was required, involving a minimum of thirty-two new pages.

The original *Big Book of John Deere Tractors* has proven itself probably the world's bestselling vintage tractor book, having passed 125,000 copies sold in its English-language version (with separate hardbound American and United Kingdom versions), in addition to a softbound Canadian edition and translations into German as *Das Grosse Buch der John Deere Traktoren*, French as *Le Grand Livre des Tracteurs John Deere*, and a new edition in Czech. An update was especially timely, since the hardbound versions in English have sold out, and the opportunity to give the book a facelift was appropriate.

With the end of Deere's arrangements with Zetor on the 2000 Series and with Renault for the 3010 and 3010SE Series, this left the way clear for new 2000 and 3000 Series low-horsepower models in the 18- to 48-hp sizes. Introduction in 2000 of the largest of the 4000 Series, the 48-hp 4700, saw the completion of this series.

For the 2000 season, the 8000/T Series was upgraded to the 9010/T Series with four models in each type: the 185-PTO-hp 8010/T, 185-hp 8210/T, 205-hp 8310/T, and 235-hp 8410/T. Engine horsepower ratings for these were 195, 215, 235, and 270, respectively.

In addition, the Yanmar-engined, three-cylinder, 30-hp 790 Advantage model had been introduced in 1998, and a 990 Advantage model was added in 2000 in the United States; two- or four-wheel drive was optional on both models, with differential lock and power steering on the four-wheel-drive and two-wheel-drive 990. The 990 had a

Yanmar, four-cylinder, 40.4-hp engine. Two other Advantage models were the 5105 and 5205, and they had John Deere PowerTech three-cylinder engines of 45 and 53 hp. The PTO horsepower of the three models was 35, 40, and 48, respectively.

4700 with aerator.

8310/T.

8410.

990 with disc.

5205 with a 521 front-end loader.

Top: *6010SE Series four-cylinder.*

Bottom: *6403/6603 Advantage.*

5020 Series, 2001–

Early in 2001, the 5020 Series Utility models replaced the 5010 Series. These were the 45-PTO-hp 5220, 55-hp 5320, 65-hp 5420, and the large 75-hp 5520 with a choice of a new deluxe cab, a new isolated open operator's station with its flat surface, or the original straddle-mount platform. Added to this were three narrow models for vineyard or orchard work, again with their own special cabs or open station platforms: the 5320N, 5420N, and 5520N.

6010 SE Series, 2000–

At the end of the twentieth century, and to compliment the 6010 Series, a 6010SE Series was introduced in Europe to form a lower-priced version of the premium series. This simple and economical series was made up of five four-cylinder models, including the 6010SE, 6110SE, 6210SE, 6310SE, and 6410SE; and two six-cylinder models, the 6510SE and 6610SE.

In the United States, the dealer meeting held in Albuquerque, New Mexico, in August 2001 saw the introduction of the Advantage Series four-cylinder, 85-PTO-hp 6403 and six-cylinder, 95-hp 6603.

6020 Series, 2001–

The big news at the dealer meeting in Albuquerque in August 2001 was the introduction of the 20 Series to the four-cylinder 6000 Series (as well as the 8000/T and 9000/T Series). In the new 6020 Series were the 80-engine-hp 6120, 90-hp 6220, 100-hp 6320, and 110-hp 6420, with an extra 120-hp 6420S in Europe. These were also available as open-station models or the 6020L low-profile series with 65-PTO-hp to 95-hp.

5020 Series, 2003–

In Europe, a new three-model 5020 Series was introduced in the summer of 2003, the 72-engine-hp 5620 with a naturally aspirated, four-cylinder, Stage 11–certified Saran engine, and the turbocharged, 60-hp 5720 and 68-hp 5820. These three tractors were smaller versions of the five 6020 models already announced but with a new deluxe cab with 320-degree visibility due to its curved rear quarters.

Top: *6420S.*

Bottom: *5820 chisel plowing.*

8020 Series and 9020 Series, 2001–

At the dealer meeting in Albuquerque in August 2001, the ten models in the 8020 Series replaced the 8010 Series: the 170-PTO-hp 8120/T, 190-hp 8220/T, 215-hp 8320/T, 235-hp 8420/T, and 255-hp 8520/T. There were also eight models in the 9020 Series: the 280-engine-hp 9120/T, 325-hp 9220/T, 375-hp 9320/T, 425-hp 9420/T, and the largest John Deere tractor up to that point, the 450-hp 9520/T. All the 8020 and 9020 tractors had features like Independent Link Suspension and ActiveSeat to give farmers a more comfortable and productive day in the field.

Announced at a dealer meeting in Columbus, Ohio, in August 2003, and partially inspired by two competitors launching similar machines, the 500-engine-hp 9620 was presented ahead of its official March 2004 due date.

In late summer of 2005, the needs of a niche market were met when the 9320, 9420, and 9520 were made into scraper specials.

Top: *9620 at work with a disc.*

Bottom: *8520/T.*

4000 Ten Series, 2002–

9420/T.

Early in 2002, nine new 4000 Ten Series models were introduced, divided into small-, mid-, and large-chassis versions. The small-chassis models were the 18.5-engine-hp 4010, the 20-hp 4110, and the 24-hp 4115, with 14, 17, and 20 PTO hp, respectively. Mid-chassis models included the 28-hp 4210, 32-hp 4310, and 35-hp 4410 with 23, 27, and 29 PTO hp. The three large-chassis models were the 4510, 4610, and 4710 with 39/33, 44/37, and 48/41 hp, respectively. This new method of judging the size by chassis type was to be transferred to the 2000, 3000, and 4000 series in due course. In Europe, the 4210 and 4510 were not marketed.

7020 Series, 6015 Series, and 2000 Series, 2002–

During the summer of 2002, the small-chassis 7020 Series was announced. It included the 95-PTO-hp 7220, 105-hp 7320, 115-hp 7420, and 125-hp 7520. With 6.8-liter PowerTech engines rated at 2,300 rpm in the case of the two smaller models and 2,100 rpm for the two larger, the engine horsepower was 110, 125, 135, and 150, respectively.

Early in 2003, an Infinitely Variable Transmission (IVT) transmission was added to the 7710 and 7810 models.

At the same time, four new 6015 Series models were added: the four-cylinder, 72-PTO-hp 6215 and 85-hp 6415; and the six-cylinder, 95-hp 6615 and 105-hp 6715.

Late in 2002, a completely new series of compact diesel tractors in the shape of the first 2000 Series small-chassis, 23/17-hp, Yanmar-engined 2210, appeared.

In 2005, the 2210 was replaced with the 18-PTO-hp 2305.

Top: *6615 two-wheel-drive.*

Bottom: *6215-MFWD.*

7320 Tractor

7220 Tractor

Left: *7220 and 7320.*

Below: *5303.*

5003 Series, 2003–

In 2003, the first three models in the 5003 Series from Augusta, Georgia, were launched in the United States. These were the 43-PTO-hp 5103, 48-hp 5203, and 55-hp 5303, with engine horsepower of 50, 56, and 64, respectively.

At the Omaha, Nebraska, dealer meeting in 2005, the 74/64-hp 5403 was launched, the largest of the 5003 Series to date.

5015 Series, 2004–

Late in 2003 for the 2004 season, another new series, the four-model 5015 Series, was launched. This included vineyard (V) and orchard (F) versions plus a 5515 High Crop, all fitted with turbocharged Deere Tier 11 engines. The 5215 and 5315 had three cylinders; the 5415 and 5515, four cylinders. The 5415 was the only model with a naturally aspirated engine; all the rest were turbocharged, including the F, V, and High Crop.

Top: *5315 with baler.*

Bottom: *5215V with cab.*

Top: *5615F with cab and sprayer.*

Bottom: *5515 High Crop two-wheel-drive.*

7020 Series, 2004–

At the dealer meeting in Columbus, Ohio, in August 2003, the three large-chassis 7010 Series models were replaced with the 7020 Series. This included the 140-PTO-hp 7720, the 155-hp 7820, and the new 170-hp 7920. The 7610 was discontinued.

4020 Series, 2004–

By 2004, the large-chassis 4000 Series was upgraded to the 4020 Series, the four models being the 36-PTO-hp 4120, 40-hp 4320, 45-hp 4520, and 50-hp 4720. All had Deere four-cylinder, turbocharged engines and all had four-wheel drive; they produced 46.9, 52.3, and 56.5 engine hp, respectively.

In December 2007, a new compact, diesel, 40.4-hp, three-cylinder 4105 debuted.

Top: *7920 plowing.*

Middle: *4105.*

Bottom: *4520 with 400CX loader.*

Top: *5525*.

Bottom: *2520*.

5025 Series, 2004–

In October 2004, four new 5025 Series utility tractors were introduced: the 45-PTO-hp 5225, 55-hp 5325, 65-hp 5425, and 75-hp 5525. Their engine horsepower was 56, 67, 81, and 91, respectively

2020 Series, 2005–

In September 2005, the 24-enqine-hp 2320 and 26.5-hp 2520 were introduced in the 2020 Series.

3020 Series, 2005–

In 2005, four 3020 Series tractors were introduced as the new mid-chassis models. They were the 29.5-engine-hp 3120, 32.4-hp 3320, 37.7-hp 3520, and 43.4-hp 3720, all with four-wheel drive as standard and three-cylinder Yanmar engines, the latter two turbocharged.

In 2006, the 32/24-hp 3203 was announced at the Omaha, Nebraska, dealer meeting.

Early in 2008, the mid-chassis, 27-engine-hp 3005 arrived.

Top: *3203 mowing with Frontier RC1060.*

Left: *3203.*

Top: *8430.*

Left: *8430T.*

8030 Series, 2005–

At the annual dealer meeting at Fort Worth, Texas, in August 2005, the following five 8030 Series models were announced: the 180-PTO-hp 8130/T, 200-hp 8230/T, 235-hp 8330/T, 255-hp 8430/T, and 277-hp 8530/T. When tested at Nebraska, the 8430/T proved to be the most fuel-efficient tractor ever tested there.

6030 Series and 7030 Series, 2006–

At the 2006 Omaha dealer meeting, the key announcement was the introduction of the 30 Series for both the 6000 and 7000 mid-range tractors from Mannheim and Waterloo. For the United States, the 6030 Series consisted of the 75-PTO-hp 6230, 85-hp 6330, and 95hp 6430, while the 7030 Series included the 140-hp 7630, 152-hp 7730, 16S-hp 7830, and 150-hp 7930.

At the Cincinnati, Ohio, dealer meeting in August 2007, the dealers saw the six regular 6030 and 7030 models, and four 7030 premium versions: the 75-PTO-hp 6230, 85-hp 6330, 95-hp 6430, 100-hp 7130, 110-hp 7230, and 125-hp 7330, plus the same premium 7030 Series with the addition of the 140-hp 7430.

Top: *6430.*

Above: *6330 Regular.*

Far left: *8530 with a veteran Model D.*

Top: *20A.*

Bottom: *100F.*

5003 Series and greenhouse and nursery tractors, 2007–

In 2007, there were thirty-two new tractors announced by Deere. It commenced with two 82-PTO-hp, 99-engine-hp 5603 and 5625 models, representing the value and premium markets, according to the special brochure covering the announcement.

During the summer of 2007, a new 5003 Series appeared: the 38-PTO-hp 5103, 47-hp 5203, 55-hp 5303, and 64-hp 5403, following the 5603.

Cincinnati, Ohio, was the chosen venue for the dealer meeting in August 2007, where four new greenhouse and nursery tractors were revealed: first, a 17-PTO-hp, 21-engine-hp 20A, and then the 76-hp 76F, S3-hp 85F, and 96-hp 100F with PTO horsepower of 66, 73, and 83, respectively.

5603 AND 5625 SERIES TRACTORS

9030 Series, 2007–

The largest models launched at the Cincinnati, Ohio, dealer meeting in August 2007 were the eight 9030 Series tractors. These included the 325-hp 9230, 375-hp 9330, 425-hp 9430/T, 475-hp 9530/T, and 530-hp 9630/T, the 9120 having been discontinued.

Chinese tractors and combines, 2007–

Deere started building combines in China in 1997, followed by tractors in the 60- to 120-hp class in Tianjin. Now in 2007, the acquisition of the new 200,000-square-meter factory at Benye allowed construction of smaller 20- to 50-hp tractors required in much of China.

Top: *9630.*

Bottom: *5603 and 5625 brochure.*

5D Series, 5E Series, 5E Limited Series, and 6D Series, 2008–

A new method of numbering both models and series was announced in 2008 with the 5D, 5E, 5E Limited, and 6D Series. The 5D Series offered two-wheel-drive only, including the 45-hp 5045D and 55-hp 5055D.

The 5E Series had optional two-wheel drive or MFWD, and it included the 45-hp 5045E, 55-hp SOSSE, 65-hp 5065E, and 75-hp 5075E, with 37-, 45-, 53-, and 61-PTO-hp engines, respectively.

The three new 5E Limited tractors were the 83-hp 5083E-L, 93-hp 5093E-L, and 101-hp 5101E-L, with PTO horsepower of 65, 75, and 82, respectively.

The four 6D models were the 100-hp 6100D, 115-hp 6115D, 130-hp 6130D, and 140-hp 6140D with PTO horsepower of 82, 95, 105, and 115, respectively. All offered optional two-wheel drive or MFWD.

Top: *5101EL.*

Bottom: *5055D.*

Left: *5065E.*

Bottom: *5045D.*

5R Series, 2008–

In Europe, the 5R Series was announced in 2008. This was the premium version of the 5045 Series and consisted of three models: the 5080R, 5090R, and 5100R. All offered four-cylinder, turbocharged engines with active-charge air cooler.

3E Series and 2C Series, 2008–

Finally in 2008, two new 3E models arrived in October; they were the 31-hp 3032E and 37-hp 3038E. Both had Detroit diesel engines, MFWD, and power steering standard with hydrostatic transmissions.

In Europe, the 37.1-engine-hp 3036E was announced with the 18.8-engine-hp 20C and 24.1-hp 25C models built in Italy.

Top: *5100R.*

Bottom: *3036E.*

5100R, 5090M, and 5090G tractors.

5D Series, 2009–

In 2009, India began following the new numbering system with the introduction of its first model, the 38-hp 5038D with optional manual or power steering. Of the twelve models available from 2008, only the two largest—the 65-engine-hp 5410 and 75-hp 5610-MFWD—had turbocharged engines; the rest were all direct-injection. The models ranged from the 35-hp Economy 5103 to the 55-hp 5310-MFWD.

5G and 5M Series, 2009–

Deere launched the new 5G and 5M series in August 2009 at a Berlin, Germany, presentation.

Top: *5090G tractor with 568 round baler.*

Middle: *5090M.*

Bottom: *5070M.*

Top: *5GV.*

Top right: *5M Series cab.*

Middle: *5M Series controls.*

Bottom: *5070M.*

Above: *5090M tractor with 328A.*

Above left: *5100GF.*

Above right: *5090G with 324A mower.*

Bottom left: *5G Series tractor cab.*

Opposite: *5090M tractor with 583 loader.*

8R Series, 2009–

John Deere launched the new 8R series in August 2009 at a Berlin, Germany, presentation.

Top: *8345R.*

Bottom: *8320RT.*

Top: *8320RT.*

Middle: *8345R.*

Bottom left: *8320R.*

Bottom right: *8320R.*

8245R.

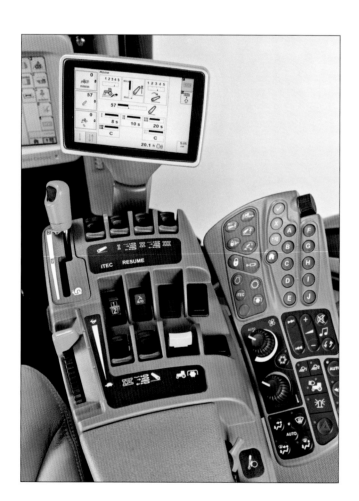

8R tractor cab.

8R tractor cab.

8345R.

8320R.

Index

Acknowledgments

The contributions of many people helped in the compiling of *The Big Book of John Deere Tractors* over the past couple years.

My thanks first to Andrew Morland, who coped nobly with my requests for more than 500 slides of brochures and photos of the real thing.

John Bridger and his son-in-law William Andrews provided more than 200 photographs of John's massive collection of Deere toys. These were supplemented by John Westerveld from the Netherlands with images of his homemade scale models.

Deere & Company's archives in East Moline, and Archivist Les Stegh in particular, was a backup source necessary in a work of this kind. Don Huber was again my reference at Moline headquarters.

In addition, the archives in Mannheim, Germany, provided many of the European facts, figures, and photographs, either directly or through the good offices of Steve Mitchell of Pharo Communications in the United Kingdom. My contacts in Mannheim were Hans Hetterich and his assistant, Christine Nagler.

From the rest of the Deere world, photos and brochures were received from Christian Hoel and Jean-François Pierre in France; Eloy Galvan Garcia in Spain; Alberto Souto in Argentina; Arthur Browning in South Africa; Danny Geller of the Australian branch; and Mr. Schneider from SLC in Brazil. The restored Chamberlain tractor photos and serial number information came from Philip Wyndham in Western Australia. Richard and Carol Hain of *Green Magazine* were their usual helpful selves.

I express my thanks to many individuals who provided information and photos from all over the world, in particular Alan Mole and Walter Reiff for Lanz information; Rune Felth and Kenny Layher for photos of the Swedish GMW tractors, and Randy Leffingwell for his photographs.

I hope I have acknowledged the many others, too numerous to mention by name here, in the captions referring to their tractors.

Michael Dregni and the team at Voyageur Press deserve a warm note of appreciation for their work on this book. Computers have taken much of the drudgery out of producing a book, but they have not eliminated the need for teamwork.

To all involved in this production—the many collectors, John Deere personnel, Voyageur Press staff, and anyone I have forgotten to mention—a very big thank you.

Don Macmillan
May 1999

About the Author and Photographers

Don Macmillan is one of the world's most respected authorities on Deere & Company. He bought his first Deere tractor in 1943, was appointed the first Deere dealer in the United Kingdom in 1958, and went on to establish one of the world's foremost collections of Deere tractors and memorabilia.

Working with Deere & Company, he authored *John Deere Tractors & Equipment* volumes 1 and 2 and *John Deere Tractors Worldwide*, all published by the American Society of Agricultural Engineers. He also contributed to *This Old Tractor*, published by Voyageur Press.

He lives in Devizes, Wiltshire, England.

Andrew Morland is the co-author with Robert N. Pripps of *Vintage Ford Tractors* and *The Field Guide to Vintage Farm Tractors* and with Nick Baldwin of *Classic Tractors of the World*, all published by Voyageur Press.

He lives in a thatched cottage in Somerset, England, that was built in the 1680s.

Randy Leffingwell is the author and photographer of *The American Farm Tractor*, *John Deere Farm Tractors*, *Caterpillar*, and several other automotive and tractor histories.

He lives in Ojai, California, USA.